Four Centuries
of
Virginia Christmas

Four Centuries of Virginia Christmas

To Bob —
Merry Christmas 2003 !

mm Theobald

by
Mary Miley Theobald and Libbey Hodges Oliver

ISBN 0-87517-112-5
Library of Congress Card Number: 00-105627

The Dietz Press
Richmond, Virginia

Table of Contents

Introduction

"*In the beginning, all America was Virginia.*" So wrote the colonial aristocrat William Byrd II in the early part of the eighteenth century.[1] No one at the time thought this statement an idle boast. Educated people knew that when England laid claim to most of North America in the fifteen hundreds, the colony named for "the Virgin Queen" swept grandly from Atlantic to Pacific. Never mind that no one had any idea what lay in between these two oceans or that

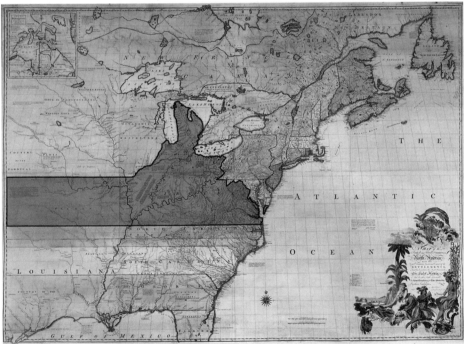

John Mitchell map courtesy of the Colonial Williamsburg Foundation

The charter that King James I gave to the Virginia Company of London granted them settlement rights to all land between the 34th and 45st latitude, from North Carolina to Maine and all points of land west. The French and the Spanish, not to mention the native Americans, disputed this claim, but as late as 1783, Virginia consisted of what is now Kentucky, West Virginia, Ohio, Indiana, Illinois, Michigan, Wisconsin, and most of Minnesota. The map above shows Virginia boundaries in 1755.

British possession was more wishful thinking than actuality, the fact remains that most of the United States and even portions of Canada were once considered part of Virginia. On the edge of this vast Virginia continent, in a forlorn settlement called Jamestown, America's Christmas celebration began to take shape.

For the better part of two centuries, Christmas was largely a Virginia phenomenon. The holiday did not exist in New England nor was it observed with much interest in other northern colonies. But in Virginia, Christmas meant a fortnight of festivities stretching from Christmas Eve through New Year's Day all the way to Twelfth Night, a season that was celebrated (by those who could afford it) with lavish feasts, prodigious drinking, fox hunting, dancing, games, music—both sacred and secular, and the decorating of churches and homes. As the generations passed, Virginians handed down their treasured English traditions and added a few of their own invention: open house, Christmas gifts, Christmas guns and fireworks, and eggnog hospitality. Virginians were among the first Americans to adopt the German tradition of the decorated tree, and Virginians pioneered the naturalistic Colonial Revival Christmas decorations of the twentieth century with Williamsburg door decorations and candlelit windows.

Photo courtesy of Colonial Williamsburg Foundation

The origin of the word Christmas is Christes Maeses, Old English for Christ's Mass.

It wasn't long before a Virginia Christmas inspired envy. As early as 1746 a London magazine rhapsodized about the "universal Hospitality" and the "full Tables and open Doors" strangers could expect to find across His Majesty's largest colony.[2] Later, visions of ante-bellum gentility would enhance the image until every holiday publication paid tribute to the old Virginia Christmas.

As Virginians moved west, they carried their Christmas customs with them to Kentucky and Ohio, to Texas and California. Explorers Lewis and Clark, with barely the means to survive, managed to put together a bit of Virginia Christmas in the wilds of the Louisiana Purchase. Ordinary men and women brought their recipes, songs, and memories of Christmas celebration with them when they packed their Conestoga wagons and faced West.

On one level, this is the story of Virginia's Christmas, how its customs evolved from pagan, Roman, English, Dutch, and German precedents and how its own homegrown traditions developed. But in a larger sense, it is the story of America's Christmas, for the American celebration is rooted in Virginia.

America started in Virginia. So did its Christmas.

End Notes

1. "The Story of Virginia: An American Experience," permanent exhibit at the Virginia Historical Society.

2. "Christmas," <u>London Magazine</u>, 1746.

Chapter One

"Never more merry"
The Early Colonial Christmas

The first Virginia Christmas found the English adventurers far from home and far from merry. Although it was spring when the three English ships landed in the New World, the men neglected the fundamentals of survival in

Photo courtesy of Colonial Williamsburg Foundation

their rush to find gold and silver, and winter found them—like the grasshopper in Aesop's fable— cold and starving, dependent upon the generosity of the native Powhatan Indians for their food.

To make matters worse, that winter in Jamestown, Virginia was one of the coldest on record. Captain John Smith, a leader and chronicler of the expedition, made

"Virginia is a Country in America," wrote Captain John Smith, "that lyeth betweene the degrees of 34 and 44 of the north latitude. The bounds thereof on the East side is the great Ocean. On the South lyeth Florida: on the North nova Francia. As for the West thereof, the limits are unknowne." [1] *(Portrait from Smith's Generall Historie of Virginia, London, 1624)*

1

no mention of their first Christmas in his book, *The Generall Historie of Virginia, New-England, and the Summer Isles.* Instead, he focused on his own exploits in captivity—he had been taken prisoner by Chief Powhatan in early December, saved by Pocahontas, and released shortly after New Year's Day.

Photo courtesy of Jamestown Yorktown Foundation

The re-created seventeenth-century fort at Jamestown settlement tells the story of America's first permanent English colony. Archaeologists continue to study the remains of the original fort, situated just a few yards from this re-creation.

Captain Smith did take note of the holiday the next year, in 1608. Circumstances were little changed: the English colonists were still in dire straits and Smith was once again trapped at an Indian village. But this Christmas, it was a severe winter storm that was keeping him and his men prisoner at Kecoughtan village (now Hampton, Virginia). This Christmas, John Smith would need no dramatic rescue by a teenage girl.

> *"The next night being lodged at Kecoughtan;"* Smith wrote, *"six or seaven dayes the extreame winde, rayne, frost and snow caused us to keepe Christmas among the Salvages, where we were never more merry, nor fed on more plentie of good Oysters, Fish, Flesh, Wild-foule, and good bread; nor never had better fires in England, then in the dry smoaky houses of Kecoughtan."* [2]

There was little in the way of Christmas celebration during those early years at Jamestown—people struggling for their very existence tend to neglect anything beyond the essentials. Food and shelter were their priorities, their faith in God their mainstay. From the earliest months there was a church inside Jamestown fort and an Anglican minister, Robert Hunt, to tend to this motley flock of young men. "Good Master Hunt our Preacher," as Captain Smith called him, would certainly have celebrated holy communion on Christmas Day.

No doubt the Christmas customs that the men missed most were those involving food. At home in England, lavish feasts were the heart of the holiday, the focal point for every gathering of family and friends. Whatever their rank in society, Englishmen pursued extravagance in holiday dining: the goal was a table crowded with more elaborately prepared food than anyone could possibly taste at one sitting.

Traditionally, the English Christmas season began on Christmas Eve and lasted until Twelfth Night, or January 6th. Dur-

Photo courtesy of Colonial Williamsburg Foundation

Three ships carried the English adventurers to the New World. Two returned to England; the smallest one stayed behind to explore the Chesapeake Bay region and facilitate trade with the native Americans.

ing those days came many opportunities for feasting, drinking, dancing, games, music, and all sorts of revelry, much of it scandalously rowdy. In many parts of England, Christmas was characterized by a period of "misrule," when ordinary expectations and behaviors were turned upside down. An upperclass Englishman was expected to entertain his neighbors, great and small, with his best food and strong spirits on Christmas Day. Christmas pantomimes brought impromptu skits into the holiday; a Yule log and its accompanying

Photo courtesy of Colonial Williamsburg Foundation

Restored to the throne in 1660, King Charles II brought an end to stern Puritan rule and the repression of Christmas. Prints such as these give a glimpse of decorating practices of the day. Note the garlands of fruits and greens that drape the walls of this banquet room, the decorations that top the portraits and hang from the chandeliers, and the candles in the windows.

wassail bowl (two traditions with Scandinavian origins) made the hearth the center attraction.

> *"An English Gentleman at the opening of the great Day, had all his Tenants and Neighbours enter'd his Hall by Day-break, the strong Beer was broach'd, and with Black-Jacks [drinking vessels] went plentifully about with Toast, Sugar, Nutmeg, and good Cheshire Cheese; the Rooms were embower'd with Holly, Ivy, Cyprus, Bays, Laurel and Mistletoe, and a bouncing Christmas Log in the Chimney, glowing like the Cheeks of a Country Milkmaid..."* [3]

The English were fond, too, of decking their halls with boughs of holly (or any other plentiful green plant), bringing a bit of winter cheer into their homes, churches, inns, kitchens, and work places. Even the town streets were decorated. A half-century before Columbus brought news of a New World across the sea, Englishmen were indulging in their love of outdoor Christmas decoration. Upright timbers or poles called standards were erected in the street and adorned with greenery at this festive time of year.

"At the Ledenhall in Cornhill . . . a standard of tre was set in myddys of the pavement fast in the grounde, nayled with holme [live oak] and Ive, for disport of Cristmasse to the peple of the Cite." [4]

John Stow, the Elizabethan historian, described in 1598 how London looked:

"Against the Feast of Christmas, every mans house, as also their parish Churches, were decked with Holm, Ivy, Bayes, and whatsoever the season of the yeere aforded to be greene. The Conduits [fountains] and Standards in the streetes were, likewise, garnished." [5]

The tradition of decking the halls with evergreen boughs is shrouded in the mists of time. The practice is mentioned in the Old Testament (Isaiah 60:13 and Nehemiah 8:15). Imperial Romans celebrated Saturnalia in December and also the new year, known as the Kalends of January, by adorning their homes with laurel and evergreens and giving evergreen branches as a good luck token for the coming year.

Some of the early Christian leaders tried to abolish such dangerous relics of heathenism. At least one bishop issued a stern edict outlawing all decorations. "Let it not be allowed to adorn the houses with laurel or with the greenery of trees," he decreed in AD 575.[6] But the custom would not be stamped out. Perhaps it is a universal reaction to the dark, dreary days of winter . . . after all, who wouldn't think of freshening the

Photo courtesy of Museum of American Frontier Culture

An English farmhouse from 1690, brought to Virginia's Frontier Culture Museum in Staunton and rebuilt, is appropriately decorated for Christmas in the northern English manner. Garlands made from sprigs of holly and herbs tied to a rope are strung around the room; holly and berries line the windowsills and garnish the platters of holiday food.

house with the sweet scent of pine or cedar, lifting everyone's spirits with the reminder that the short winter days had started to stretch into spring?

Decorating for Christmas with greenery persisted throughout the Middle Ages and into Renaissance Europe. The Church, accepting what it could not change, gave these pagan practices a Christian metaphor. Holly now symbolized the crown of thorns; its berries the drops of blood on Christ's brow. German, Italian, English, and other period accounts provide ample evidence that decorating with evergreens and sweet-smelling herbs was a widespread custom, one that knew no national boundaries.

Photo courtesy of Colonial Williamsburg Foundation

This scene illustrates one way English families celebrated Christmas: with greenery on the mantel and spirits on the table. (Detail from "Christmas Gambols," London, 1780)

With holly and ivy so green and so gay,
We deck up our houses as fresh as the day;
With bays and rosemary, and laurel compleat,
And every one now is a king in conceit.
(Poor Robin's Almanack, 1695)[7]

As soon as tobacco had set the struggling Virginia colony on its feet, life became marginally liveable—even comfortable for the fortunate few. Landowners could afford to indulge in holiday observances, and many of the old English Christmas customs were transplanted to Virginia's fertile soil.

In 1686 a French Huguenot named Durand was travelling through the colonies, recording his observances in a journal. Shortly before Christmas,

Photo courtesy of Colonial Williamsburg Foundation

*T*heir dusky green color and spicy fragrance give bayberry candles a natural association with Virginia Christmas. The timing is right, as well. Berries of the bayberry plant (also called myrtle berries or candle berries) mature in November and December, allowing those who made bayberry candles to have a supply right before the holidays.

To make candles of any sort involved a good deal of work but with bayberry candles, there was the extra chore of gathering buckets full of tiny bayberries from the native bushes. Bayberry grows wild and plentiful along the eastern coastal regions of America but its berries are small and tedious to collect. First the berries are boiled in hot water until the oil floats to the top. This is skimmed off into another vessel and the boiling repeated. The oil hardens into a dirty green wax that can be dipped or poured into candlemolds. For their trouble, the colonists had a candle with a long life and a very pleasant scent.

Making candles from bayberries was new to the colonists. Robert Beverley, an early Virginia planter, wrote of the "very modern" discovery in 1705, sounding almost like a very modern advertisement.

"At the Mouth of their Rivers, and all along upon the Sea and Bay, and near many of their Creeks and Swamps, grows the Myrtle, bearing a Berry, of which they make a hard brittle Wax, of a curious green Colour, which by refining becomes almost transparent. Of this they make Candles, which are never greasie to the Touch, nor melt with lying in the hottest Weather: Neither does the Snuff of these ever offend the Smell, like that of a Tallow-Candle; but instead of being disagreeable, if an Accident puts a Candle out, it yields a pleasant Fragrancy to all that are in the Room; insomuch that nice People often put them out, on purpose to have the Incense of their expiring Snuff." [8]

Candles of any sort were used far less than is generally thought. The cost of candles meant that most people used them infrequently or not at all. A large room in a wealthy plantation home was pronounced "luminous and splendid" when there were "four very large candles burning on the table where we supp'd, three others in different parts of the Room." [9] Candles did not appear on dining tables unless the meal was served after dark.

he stopped at the home of Colonel William Fitzhugh, "whose houses stand along the banks of the great Pethomak [Potomac] river." There he was treated to a lavish celebration.

> *"The Christmas holidays were drawing near . . . He [Fitzhugh] treated us royally, there was good wine and all kinds of beverages, so there was a great deal of carousing. He had sent for three fiddlers, a jester, a tight-rope dancer, an acrobat who tumbled around, and they gave us all the entertainment one could wish for."* [10]

William Fitzhugh was one of the most successful planters in Virginia and his extravagance was typical only of the emerging upper class. In their eagerness to imitate English lords, other wealthy plantation owners entertained in a similar manner. William Byrd, a large landowner and faithful diarist, enjoyed celebrating Christmas with friends. He describes several Christmases like this one in 1709:

Photo courtesy of Colonial Williamsburg Foundation

Westover was the home of the Byrds, one of the most important early Virginia families. The Georgian style house pictured above was built around 1730 by William Byrd II whose secret diaries—once decoded—shed much light on the lifestyle of the colonial elite, including their celebration of Christmas.

"Then we went to church, notwithstanding it rained a little, where Mr. Anderson preached a good sermon for the occasion. I received the Sacrament with great devoutness. After church the same company went to dine with me . . . Then we took a walk about the plantation . . . In the evening we were merry with nonsense and so were my servants." [11]

Over the Christmas season, Byrd's guests came and went. They played billiards and cards, danced, drank wine, "slid and skated on the ice," and enjoyed festive dinners. The Byrd servants and slaves celebrated as well.

"I inquired of my people how everything was and they told me well. Then I gave them some rum and cider to be merry with . . ." [12]

Most colonists could only aspire to such excess. For the vast majority of Virginians, Christmas probably meant no more than a worship service at church, if one were near, and the best food and spirits they could afford to set on the table. For the indentured servant class, Christmas rarely brought more than a welcome respite from work and an extra ration of food and drink.

And the slaves? Many, if not most, of Virginia's slaves during the seventeenth century had been born and raised in Africa and brought to North America with little more than what they carried in their heads. Colonial masters had mixed feelings about introducing Christianity to their slaves—some feared that Christianity and slavery were incompatible (at least until 1667 when an act was passed assuring slaveholders that baptizing their slaves would not disqualify them from bondage) while others thought

Photo courtesy of Colonial Williamsburg Foundation

Jamestown's restored Anglican church, where early colonists worshipped, is opened to the public on Jamestown Island.

it their Christian duty to give religious instruction to their "people." The Anglican clergy encouraged conversion and as the decades passed, many slaves were baptized.

For newly enslaved Africans, unfamiliar with Christianity, the only interest Christmas held was the lighter workload and the extra food. But during the second half of the colonial period, they began to develop their own distinct ways of observing the Christmas holiday.[13]

Customs in the northern colonies provided a sharp contrast to those in the South. Englishmen who first settled in Massachusetts and Connecticut brought their families with them: wives, parents, and children. They came for religious freedom and they came to stay. Early immigrants to Virginia, on the other hand, were, in large part, single young men with a single motive—get rich quick and go home. The northern colonists, called Puritans because of their desire to purify the Church of England, looked to the Bible for guidance in all human affairs. And since the Bible said nothing about celebrating Christmas, they were determined to treat the day like any other. No feasting, no revelry, not even a church service would mark the occasion unless December 25 happened to fall on a Sunday.

Plymouth's Governor William Bradford soon discovered that even pious Puritans could not wish away ancient customs. On Christmas Day, 1621, in the settlement's second year, he came across some men taking the day off to play games.

> *"He fowned them in Ye streete at play, openly; some pitching ye barr, and some at stoole ball and such like sports. So he went to them and tooke away their implements, and told them it was against his conscience that they should play, and others worke."* [14]

Enough Puritans continued to disregard the ban on Christmas that it became necessary for the church leaders to pass laws forbidding any sort of celebration. "Whosoever shall be found observing any such day as Christmas," reads one law of 1659, "either by forbearing of labor, feasting, or any other way . . . shall pay for every such offence five shillings." When this punishment proved inadequate, imprisonment and whipping were added. In Connecticut, officials went even further, forbidding even the making of mince pie![15] Later in the century pressure from London caused such laws to be repealed but Puritan influence had, by then, effectively erased the holiday from the calendar. For New England's first two hundred years, December 25 was just another wintery day.

To be fair, the Puritans had several good reasons to try to legislate Christmas out of existence. First, they argued, nowhere in the Bible is there anything to suggest that Jesus was born on December 25. In fact, evidence pointed towards a date in the spring, the time of year when shepherds need to watch their flocks by night to protect the newborn lambs from predators. The Reverend Ezra Stiles, the Congregationalist minister who became president of Yale, spoke for many Puritans when he wrote, "if it had been the will of Christ that the anniversary of his birth should have been celebrated, he would at least let us have known the day." December 25, Puritan ministers charged, was nothing more than the old pagan Saturnalia with a Christian veneer. [16]

They were quite correct. Saturnalia, that week-long, raucous romp through the winter solstice, had been celebrated throughout the Roman empire in honor of Saturn, the harvest god. Early in the fourth century, church fathers decided to marry Christmas to Saturnalia, making it possible for the pagans to convert to the new religion without having to give up the fun of the old. This bargain was widely understood in colonial times—in fact, a December 1739 issue of the *Virginia Gazette* acknowledges that "the Celebration of the Feast of December. . . [was] in Use among the Romans,

Photo courtesy of Colonial Williamsburg Foundation

When in 1660, Christmas was restored along with Charles II, all but the strictest Puritans resumed their celebrations.

"Now thanks to God for Charles' return, Whose absence made old Christmas mourn; For then we scarcely did know, Whether it Christmas were or no." [17]

many Years before the Birth of our Savior Christ"—but the Puritans were all for sweeping out pagan clutter as they purified their church.[18]

The other, and probably more important, reason for banishing Christmas involved the dissolute nature of the celebrations. The day had long ago lost whatever pious overtones church leaders had hoped for; in some parts of England it had become little more than an excuse for riotous disorder, gambling, promiscuity, and drunken revelry. An English book, published around 1740, describes the old customs of Christmas beginning with "Chapter I. Of Mirth and Jollity, Christmas Gambols, Eating, Drinking, and Kissing, &c."[19] It was the 'Kissing et cetera,' that worried Puritans most.

The Reverend Cotton Mather lashed out against such excesses in 1712. "[T]he Feast of Christ's Nativity is spent in Reveling, Dicing, Carding, Masking, and in all Licentious Liberty . . . by Mad Mirth, by long Eating, by hard Drinking, by lewd Gaming, by rude Reveling . . ." as though, said others, it was some heathenish feast of Saturn or Bacchus.[20]

Photo courtesy of Colonial Williamsburg Foundation

MIDNIGHT MODERN CONVERSATION

Suppressing this sort of punch bowl brawling at Christmas time was the aim of Puritans in England and in the New England colonies. But Parliament's attempts to banish Christmas had little effect in Virginia. (Print by William Hogarth 1732-1733.)

The Puritans were not alone in their desire to banish Christmas from the calendar. Presbyterians, Methodists, Baptists, Congregationalists, Mennonites, Brethren, Amish, and Quakers shared the view that society would be better off without this degenerate holiday that dishonored Christ. When Puritans gained political supremacy in England during the middle of the seventeenth century, they did their best to abolish Christmas there as well, or at least to turn it into a day of fasting rather than feasting.

> **CHRISTMAS IN SCOTLAND**
>
> *Christmas was forbidden in Calvinist Scotland as early as 1583.*

"An ordinance for the better Observation of the Feast of the Nativity of Christ" was passed by the Puritan faction in Parliament in 1644, calling for Christmas Day "to be kept with the more solemn Humiliation, because it may call to Remembrance our Sins and the Sins of our Forefathers, who have turned this Feast, pretending the Memory of Christ, into an extreme Forgetfulness of him, by giving Liberty to carnal and sensual Delights . . ."[21]

A good attempt, perhaps, but the Puritan regime in England was short-lived and reforming the hedonistic (and remote) colony of Virginia was not one of its priorities. In colonial communities where Anglicans, Roman Catholics, Lutherans, and Moravians predominated, Christmas continued to be observed with both religious and secular celebrations.

Virginia's established Anglican church had no thought of discouraging Christmas. Mercifully, the most objectionable parts of the English celebration, such as mummers and wassailing (an aggressive form of begging), did not survive the trans-Atlantic crossing, possibly because the colony's inhabitants were so spread out as to make bands of masked ruffians drinking their way from house to house an impractical pastime. Nonetheless, Virginia was not exempt from Christmas excess, as evidenced by the newspaper editors and the Anglican ministers who took care to warn parishioners against holiday temptations. Reverend William Dawson of Bruton Parish Church in Williamsburg preached this same Christmas sermon at least four times in the 1730s.

> *"But let us take Care, that, during this Holy Season, our Joy does not degenerate into Sin and Sensuality; that we do not express it by Luxury and Intemperance, to the great Scandal of our Saviour and His holy Religion."* [22]

The pineapple motif permeates early American decorative arts. It is as much at home perched high atop the plantation houses at Shirley, above, and Brandon, right, as it is on this ceramic mold or this eighteenth-century chest. On the right, the pineapple's golden body and green leaves provide the inspiration for a naturalistic teapot.

HISTORY OF THE PINEAPPLE

*E*uropeans have been fascinated with "the mysterious pine-apple" ever since Christopher Columbus came into contact with this New World fruit in the West Indies. Early explorers to the islands praised them rapturously. "Pine-apples," wrote one man who sampled them during a Caribbean voyage, were "neere so bigge as an Hartichocke, but the most daintiest taste of any fruit."[23] A ship's captain who sailed to Barbados in 1657 came to the same conclusion but in far more words. After devoting three entire pages to his description of the pineapple, he finally summed it up as "certainly the nectar

which the Gods drunke; for on earth there is none like it." Samples of the delectable pineapple did not arrive in England until a hundred and fifty years after Columbus' explorations. The first one, legend has it, was presented to Oliver Cromwell during his tenure as Lord Protector. The problem was transportation. As with all fresh foods, pineapples from the New World spoiled before the ship reached its destination. The obvious solution? Bring the tropical plant to Europe and cultivate it in hot houses. The less obvious difficulty? The pineapple is hard to grow. This only added to its mystique, not to mention its cost, making the pineapple a favorite on royal dining tables and the caviar of its day.[24]

And therein lies the link between the pineapple and hospitality: serving one's guests this rare treat would certainly have been seen as a hospitable gesture. However, no documentation exists for the often heard assertion that the pineapple was the symbol of hospitality during the colonial period. To be sure, it did widespread duty as a decorative element—printed onto fabrics and wallpaper, illustrated in botanical prints and paintings, and engraved onto silver hollowware—and it does make a perfect finial for a newel post, but the pineapple did not symbolize hospitality to anyone in America until well beyond the colonial period. If anything can be said to have symbolized hospitality to colonial Virginians, it would have been the punch bowl.

End Notes

1. Arber, Edward and A. G. Bradley, eds., <u>Travels and Works of Captain John Smith</u>, Vol. I, p. 47.

2. Barbour, Philip L., ed., <u>The Complete Works of Captain John Smith</u>, Vol. II, p. 194.

3. Roberts, F., <u>Round about our Coal-Fire</u>, p. 1.

4. <u>Oxford English Dictionary</u>, Vol. X, pp. 815-16.

5. Tille, Alexander, <u>Yule and Christmas, Their Place in the Germanic Year</u>, pp. 105-106.

6. Ibid., p. 103.

7. <u>The Christmas Book: Christmas in the Olden Time: its customs and their Origin</u>, p. 31.

8. Wright, Louis B., ed., <u>History and Present State of Virginia</u>, pp. 137-38.

9. Goodwin, Mary R. M., "Christmas in Colonial Virginia," p. xxiii.

10. Chinard, Gilbert, ed., <u>A Huguenot Exile in Virginia</u>, pp. 156-161.

11. Byrd, William, <u>Diary of William Byrd II</u>, Dec. 25, 1709.

12. Ibid., Dec. 25, 1711.

13. Turner, John, "Freeing Religion Resource Book," p. 169.

14. Harris, Brayton, "Christmas," <u>Virginia</u>, (Winter 1993).

15. Cox, James A., "Saving Christmas in the Colonies," <u>Colonial Williamsburg Journal</u>, (Winter 1990-91), p. 15; and Brayton Harris, "Christmas," <u>Virginia</u>, (Winter 1993).

16. Nissenbaum, Stephen, <u>The Battle for Christmas</u>, p. 36. The authors are generally indebted to Mr. Nissenbaum for his insight into the transformation of Christmas celebration from hooliganism to child-centered family holiday. His excellent book is well worth reading.

17. Rawlings, Kevin, <u>We Were Marching on Christmas Day</u>, p. 12.

18. <u>Virginia Gazette</u> (Purdie & Dixon), December 14-21, 1739.

19. Roberts, F. <u>Round about our Coal-Fire</u>, p. 1.

20. Nissenbaum, <u>The Battle for Christmas</u>, p. 7.

21. Goodwin, "Christmas in Colonial Virginia," p. 2.

22. Turner, John, "A Sedate, Rational, and Manly Pleasure," <u>Interpreter</u>, (Winter 1998-99), p. 5.

23. Barbour, <u>The Complete Works of Captain John Smith</u>, p. 232.

24. Olmert, Michael, "The Hospitable Pineapple," <u>Colonial Williamsburg Journal</u>, (Winter 1997-98) pp. 46-57.

Chapter Two

"Universal Hospitality Reigns" The Eighteenth-Century Virginia Christmas

The mystique of the Virginia Christmas took hold during the eighteenth century. It was rooted in the extraordinary hospitality shown to strangers and family alike.

> *"The inhabitants are very Courteous to Travellers," wrote Robert Beverley in 1705. "A Stranger has no more to do, but to inquire upon the Road, where any Gentleman, or good House-keeper Lives, and there he may depend upon being received with Hospitality. This good Nature is so general among their People, that the Gentry when they go abroad, order their Principal Servant to entertain all Visitors, with every thing the Plantation affords. And the poor Planters, who have but one Bed, will very often sit up, or lie upon a Form or Couch all Night, to make room for a weary Traveller, to repose himself after his Journey."* [1]

English traveller Nicholas Cresswell (who may well have been a British spy) thought that Virginians were:

> *"the most hospitable people on earth. If a stranger went amongst them, no matter of what country, if he behaved decently, had a good face, a good coat and a tolerable share of good-nature, would dance with the women and*

drink with the men, with a little adulation—of which, by the way, they are very fond—with these qualifications he would be entertained amongst them with the greatest friendship as long as he pleased to stay." [2]

The influential *London Magazine* published an article in 1746 marvelling at the gracious welcome travellers received in this, his Majesty's largest and most populous colony. Later, this would come to be called "Southern Hospitality."

"All over the Colony, an universal Hospitality reigns, full Tables and open Doors, the kind Salute, the generous Detention . . . Strangers are fought after with Greediness, as they pass the Country, to be invited." [3]

The great distances between Virginia plantations and the difficulty of travelling between them best explain this welcoming attitude. In a society where people lived isolated from others for most of the year, the holiday season meant visiting. Friends, relatives, and even strangers broke the monotony of daily life and filled the evenings with lively conversation.

VIRGINIA ALMANACK FOR THE YEAR OF OUR LORD GOD 1764

"Now Christmas comes, 'tis fit that we
Should feast and sing, and merry be
Keep open house, let fiddlers play
A fig for cold, sing care away
And may they who thereat repine
On brown Bread and on small beer dine."

Christmas was the height of the social season for good reason. In Virginia, as in any agricultural society, winters were a time of rest. The crops had been harvested; spring planting was months away. Food was plentiful—and so was the homemade ciders, beer, and wines. December was the traditional time for slaughtering as well as for harvesting oysters from the Chesapeake Bay, so fresh meat and shellfish were abundant. Tidewater Virginia has long been blessed with mild winters, making travel by horse, carriage, or small boat relatively easy. At Christmastime, homes great and small bulged with house guests. Visits lasting weeks or even months were not uncommon among gentry families; nearer neighbors rode over for the day and returned home to their own beds at night.

During the eighteenth century, Christmas was an adult holiday in which children played no significant part. It was a season rather than a single day, a series of social gatherings that began a few days before December 25 and lasted through New Year's Day until Twelfth Night (January 6), a day known on the church calendar as Epiphany. Some stretched the celebration to Candlemas, February 2, the last day of the Christmas cycle (now our Groundhog's Day). An irreverent rhyme in one Virginia Almanac pokes fun at the elasticity of the season:

> *"When New Year's Day is past and gone,*
> *Christmas is with some people done,*
> *But further some will it extend,*
> *And at Twelfth Day their Christmas end.*
> *Some people stretch it further yet,*
> *At Candlemas they finish it.*
> *The gentry carry it further still*
> *And finish it just when they will;*
> *They drink good wine and eat good chear*
> *And keep their Christmas all the Year.* [4]

Whatever its length, Christmas was a time of extended visits between family and friends, a time of elaborate feasts and excessive drinking, a time to enjoy as much entertainment as hosts and hostesses could devise. Jefferson called it a "day of greatest mirth and jollity."

"Nothing is now to be heard of in conversation, but the Balls, the Fox-hunts, the fine entertainments, and the good fellowship, which are to be exhibited at the approaching Christmas," wrote Philip Vickers Fithian, tutor to the Carter children of Nomini Hall in Westmoreland County.[5] Taking part in the

VIRGINIA ALMANACK FOR THE YEAR OF OUR LORD GOD 1772

"Christmas is come, hang on the pot,
Let spits turn round and ovens be hot
Beef, pork, and poultry now provide
To feast thy neighbours at this tide.
Then wash all down with good wine and beer
And so with Mirth conclude the Year."

Christmas festivities of one of Virginia's wealthiest gentry families meant that Fithian would experience the most lavish holiday of his life. Common folk— the "middling sort" as they were called—adapted the celebrations to their own circumstances, participating in Christmas entertainments on a more modest scale or not at all.

Balls

Virginians, said the Reverend Andrew Burnaby with a trace of disapproval, were "immoderately fond of dancing."[6] Many a small gathering was spontaneously transformed into a dancing party—all that was needed was a source of music and a few moments to clear the floor of furniture. In Virginia's humid climate, crowded rooms and physical exertion were most happily combined in the cool months, making Christmas a most agreeable time for formal balls.

Photo courtesy of Colonial Williamsburg Foundation
Virginians, just as their English counterparts depicted in "A Family Group," enjoyed learning the latest dances. (Detail from painting by Charles Phillips, circa 1730.)

Dancing lessons were an important part of a young person's education and no occasion better demonstrated one's accomplishments than a Christmas ball. While musicians supplied the tunes, guests danced the intricate steps of minuets, jigs, country dances, cotillions, and reels like the popular "Sir Roger de Coverley," which came to be known as the Virginia Reel.

Black musicians, slave or free, were usually preferred for such occasions, their fiddle music leading the revelers long into the early morning hours. One of the most prominent fiddlers of the late colonial period was Sy Gilliat. Formerly slave or servant to Governor Norborne Berkeley, Baron de Botetourt,

> *"The Gentm. and Ladies here are perfectly well bred, not an ill Dancer in my Govmt." (Governor William Gooch, Dec. 28, 1727)*[7]

during the years before the Revolution, Sy's reputation moved easily from Williamsburg to Richmond, where he and his fiddle were in constant demand.

> *"He was tall," recollected one Richmonder, "and even in his old age, (if he ever grew old), erect and dignified. When he appeared officially in the orchestra, his dress was an embroidered silk coat and vest of faded lilac, small clothes (he would not say breeches,) and silk stockings . . . This court-dress was coeval with the reign of Lord Botetourt, and probably part of the fifty suits which, (according to the inventory he left) constituted his wardrobe; to complete this court costume, Sy. wore a brown wig with side curls and a long queue appended. His manners were as courtly as his dress, and he elbowed himself and his fiddle-stick through the world with great propriety and harmony."* [8]

At a break in the dancing around midnight, the dancers would be led to another room for the evening's colorful climax: a magnificent dessert table crowded with platters, plates, baskets, bowls, glasses, and pyramids of delictable sweets and beverages. Suitably refreshed, most would dance 'til dawn. On occasion, a grand ball might continue on for several days.

Fox Hunting

Fox hunting was a favorite Christmas pastime of Virginia's gentry. George Washington's journal entries mention the sport at least once at every Mount Vernon Christmas. "Went fox Hunting and kill'd a fox in Company with the two Mr. Triplet's and Mr. Peake, who dined here," he wrote on December 27, 1770. [9]

The hunt usually started at dawn. The wily grey fox was the preferred quarry. Virginians called foxes "vermin" and considered they were doing a good deed to rid the countryside of such troublesome pests.

Christmas Guns

"I was waked this morning by Guns fired all round the House," wrote Philip Fithian with some surprise.[10] It was Christmas morning 1773, his first in the South, and the young tutor from New Jersey was evidently not familiar with the Virginia custom of firing Christmas guns. Some called it "shooting in Christmas," or, when the commotion was repeated a week later, "shooting in the New Year."

The origin of the custom is not known but it may have started as a way of communicating with distant neighbors, a form of Christmas greeting. The boys loaded their guns with powder only, so as not to waste expensive lead. It was *not* an old English tradition.

Photo courtesy of Colonial Williamsburg Foundation

Detail from "Shooting" after a painting by Geo. T. Stubbs, London, 1779.

Mistletoe

Hunting mistletoe occupied boys and young men. This parasitic evergreen grows high in hardwood trees, about two-thirds of the way up. When the tree's leaves are green, the mistletoe hides in its lofty branches, invisible to the most discerning eye, but by December, all the deciduous leaves have fallen. The tree is bare and the green mistletoe exposed—just in time for the Christmas season.

Searching the woods for mistletoe could occupy the boys for some time. If it was found growing too high in the tree for climbing, they would make a game of shooting it down. The sport required good aim but the rewards were considerable. By long custom, anyone caught standing beneath a piece of

Published as the Act directs, by Bentley & Cº. Jan,1,1791.

CHRISTMAS IN THE COUNTRY.

This late eighteenth-century English print shows the rollicking behavior all too common during the Christmas season. Note the drunk with the chamber pot on his head and the boy pouring his drink into another's pocket. The large bunch of mistletoe hanging from the rafters has induced one amorous couple to indulge in a favorite pastime. Notice, too, the holly sprigs in the windowpanes.

mistletoe hung inside the house must forfeit a kiss. Today, in rural Virginia shooting down mistletoe is still a popular Christmas diversion.

Games

In colonial times, gambling (like horse racing) was a gentleman's privilege not extended to the "lower orders"—the craftsmen, laborers, servants, and apprentices who were supposed to be working, not wasting their time with betting games. But at Christmas, the laws relaxed, allowing most people to indulge legally in this upper class pastime.

Male and female, young and old, Virginia's gentry wagered often but usually not excessively. This was not London where thousands of pounds might change hands on the strength of one card. Most adults laid paltry bets on cards, dice, and board games and many who kept diaries or daily account books, like Washington and Jefferson, recorded their gains and losses with careful precision. Many children gambled. Little Sally Fairfax of Toulston Plantation in Fairfax County happily recorded in her diary that she won ten shillings at Christmas.

Card games with names like whist (a forerunner to modern bridge),

Photo courtesy of Colonial Williamsburg Foundation

DECEMBER.   DECEMBRE.

Card playing, a popular pastime among colonial Virginians of all ages and ranks, usually involved wagers. Note the vase of holly on the mantel. Print is by Carington Bowles, London, 1780.

Playing the Game at QUADRILLE*, from an Original Painting in Vauxhall Gardens.*

Print is from a painting by Francis Hayman, circa 1750.

piquet (similar to rummy), and loo were favored by the gentry; all-fours and put (the ancestor to our poker) were generally considered vulgar games, unsuitable for gentlemen or ladies. Cribbage, backgammon, dice games, and board games such as "The Royall and Most Pleasant Game of the Goose" were popular. Some large plantation owners, like William Byrd, had their own billiards tables. Only men played such games in public taverns but in private homes, women played too, especially when there was company.

Adults and young people played kissing games and other indoor games that today would be considered childish. At one Christmas party at Nomini Hall, about twenty young people finished their dancing, then "at the proposal of several, (with Mr. Carter's approbation) we played Button, to get Pauns for Redemption. . . in the course of redeeming my Pauns, I had several Kisses of the Ladies! . . . Soon as we rose from supper, the Company form'd into a semicircle round the fire" and embarked upon another game, this one with the charming name of Break the Pope's Neck. [11]

Outdoor games were limited in the winter but guests might go horseback riding on a fine day. Ice skating on frozen ponds, with or without skates, meant an energetic diversion for adults as well as children. In Norfolk ice skates could be purchased from the merchants Balfour and Barraud, in Williamsburg from Sarah Pitt's millinery shop; however, skates were not necessary for taking "a slide on the ice."

Whatever the age of the guests, impromptu reading or pantomimes of proverbs became the rage in the early years of the eighteenth century. William Byrd of Westover in Charles City County probably introduced this amusement to Virginia, having learned it in London—his diary mentions a Twelfth Night party at Westover where a dozen friends acted out little plays until one in the morning. Longer plays might be read aloud with a different guest taking each part or even performed with makeshift costumes, music, and props. Reading aloud from novels, romances, poems, and "improving literature" also passed the time agreeably. [12]

Music

Everyone was fond of music—especially when it highlighted the accomplishments of marriageable young ladies and gentlemen, all of whom were expected to sing or to perform credibly upon some instrument. Well-to-do gentry families hired music teachers for their children. Most families owned at least one instrument, often a harpsichord, guitar, fiddle, or recorder. Music teachers who traveled between plantations or set up shop in Alexandria, Fredericksburg, Williamsburg, Norfolk, or Richmond seemed to have little difficulty finding pupils.

Musical instruments were by no means limited to the upper class. Williamsburg craftsman James Geddy was prosperous enough to afford a spinet

Photo courtesy of Colonial Williamsburg Foundation

for his daughter Anne, and flutes and whistles were within reach of most. Slaves were known to play fiddles or French horns for their master's entertainments, as well as homemade banjos, drums, and other percussion instruments for their own amusement. Ladies generally preferred the spinet or harpsichord, gentlemen the violin, although no instrument was considered the exclusive domain of one gender.

One young law student who had an early reputation as a respectable violinist was Thomas Jefferson. At Christmas 1759, he took a break from his studies in Williamsburg to play violin duets with another, slightly older, student by the name of Patrick Henry. Jefferson's talent caught the interest of Governor Francis Fauquier who invited the young man to perform at the Palace on more than one occasion.

Two days before Christmas in 1773, guests to Nomini Hall in Westmoreland County (on Virginia's Northern Neck) were thoroughly charmed when their host, Councillor Robert Carter, gave an informal concert on the glass armonica. One of the wealthiest men in the colony, Carter was an avid musician—he played the harpsichord, guitar, violin, piano, German flute, and organ. The glass armonica, so named by its inventor, Benjamin Franklin, consisted of

spinning glass bowls played with wet fingers. Some called it "musical glasses." Carter's instrument, ordered from London at great expense, was the only one of its kind in the entire colony. When Carter's tutor heard the music, he was clearly at a loss for words.

Photo courtesy of Colonial Williamsburg Foundation

"This evening Mr. Carter spent playing on the glass armonica; It is the first time I have heard the instrument. The music is charming. The notes are clear and inexpressibly soft, they swell, and are inexpressibly grand; and either it is because the sounds are new, and therefore please me, or it is the most captivating instrument I have ever heard." [13]

Singing

Now Christmas comes, 'tis fit that we
Should feast and sing, and merry be
Keep open House, let Fiddlers play
A fig for cold, sing Care away.

(Virginia Almanack, 1766)

Singing care away with traditional Christmas carols was another popular pastime. Carols played a significant role in home entertainments during the eighteenth century but not, interestingly, in church. Many of the old carols maintain their popularity today, including "The First Noel," "God Rest You Merry Gentlemen," "The Holly and the Ivy," "The Snow Lay on the Ground," and "I Saw Three Ships."

At church services and at home, parishioners sang hymns and psalms. Many Virginians enjoyed the hymns from the book of Dr. Isaac Watts, composer of "Joy to the World." Charles Wesley, brother to John Wesley the founder of Methodism, wrote over 7,000 hymns, among them, "Hark, the Herald Angels Sing." Philip Fithian, tutor to the Carter children who became a missionary on the western Virginia frontier, records in his journal singing for an hour on Christmas Even at the urging of his hosts in Staunton, Virginia. He sang "Mr. Watt's admirable Hymns—I myself was entertain'd; I felt myself improv'd; so much Love to Jesus is set forth—So much divine Exercise." [14]

> *"Hark! How all the welkin rings,*
> *"Glory to the King of Kings,*
> *Peace on earth and mercy mild,*
> *God and sinners reconciled."*
>
> John Wesley, Hymns and Sacred Poems

Christmas Feasts and Dessert Tables

The focal point of every holiday gathering was food and drink. For the landed gentry, Christmas Day involved a sumptuous feast with a magnificent presentation of elaborate food and strong spirits. An array of meats, game, fowl, and preserved fruits and vegetables crowded the dining table along with various preparations of fish and seafood caught in Tidewater rivers and the Chesapeake Bay. There were baked goods too, large cakes and small cakes (called cookies today), puddings, jellies, sweetmeats, candied fruits and nuts, wines and rum punches. It was an era of conspicuous consumption, when quantity meant quality and presentation mattered more than taste.

Virginians continued the English custom of inviting friends and neighbors to the Christmas feast.

Decoratively stacked pyramids of sweetmeats or small cakes appeared on festive European tables at least as early as the seventeenth century.

> *"At Christmas be mery, and thanke god of all:*
> *and feast thy pore neighbours, the great and the small.*
> *Yea al the yere long, have an eie to the poore:*
> *and god shall sende luck, to kepe open thy doore."* [15]

The main meal was served in the afternoon on an elaborately arranged table dressed with a fine white linen or damask cloth. Colonial Virginians, obsessed with symmetry in their architecture, gardens, and decorative arts, were no less conscious of their dining table design. Each dish of food was precisely balanced with a similarly sized dish on the opposite side of the table. Eighteenth-century cook books and household guides included sample menus appropriate for the season as well as charts

Cookbooks, like John Farley's London Art of Cookery and Housekeeper's Complete Assistant *(1796), often included information about ways to set a proper table along with recipes, called receipts, for each dish. This diagram recommends a menu for December when holiday entertaining was at its peak.*

showing how the fashionable hostess might arrange her table.

Between courses, guests retired to another room so that servants or slaves could clear the table and set the next course. At an important Christmas feast, two courses of desserts would usually follow two courses of meats and vegetables, the main visual difference being the absence of a tablecloth for the dessert courses. The hostess's reputation—indeed, the entire family's social standing—rose or fell according to the number of elaborate dishes on the table. Twenty or thirty was not thought excessive; more was better. Custom required the number of dishes in each course to remain the same throughout the meal. Elizabeth Raffald, the "Miss Manners" of her day, minced no words in her household guide: "as many dishes as you have in one course, so many baskets or plates your dessert [course] must have."[16]

The traditional Virginia Christmas dinner included many "New World" dishes: native turkeys and ducks, Virginia hams, venison, partridges, and oysters were plentiful on this side of the Atlantic. So was roast beef, roast goose, plum pudding, and mince pie. Some of the most popular "Old World" foods, like roast swan and peacock, or the boar's head, were absent from colonial tables.

Heavy drinking was a fundamental ingredient of the Christmas holiday, regardless of one's age, sex, social status, or condition of servitude. The tem-

Photo courtesy of Colonial Williamsburg Foundation

perance movement would not start until the next century and few saw anything amiss in bidding farewell to sobriety during the Christmas season. Alcoholic beverages like "small beer" (meaning weak in alcoholic content), cider, and wine were consumed throughout the year with every meal; during
the Christmas season, the quality and quantity of these everyday drinks would
rise. In wealthier households, drinking started early in the morning and continued throughout the day and long into the night with imported wines like
sherry, claret, madeira, port, malaga, canary, fayal, sack, lisbon, champagne,
plus stronger beverages like brandy, rum, gin, and whiskey. No "small beer"
or weak cider at Christmas time!

> *"Strong-Beer Stout Syder and a good fire*
> *Are things this season doth require."* [17]

A large bowl of punch symbolized hospitality to colonial Virginians. Every family had its favorite recipe. The word punch is thought to have originated with the Hindustani word for "five," referring to the five basic ingredients: rum, water, sugar, citrus, and spices. Omit the citrus and spices, the two
most costly ingredients, and you had a poor man's version known as "toddy."

At a formal ball, the guests were treated to a "dessert table"—a feast for
the eyes as well as the palate. Fancy cakes, syllabubs, sugared nuts, "ices,"
puddings, colorful jellies, marzipan, fruits that were dried, brandied, preserved, or candied, and other sweetmeats were
served in the family's best silver, porcelain, or glass
dishes. All were geometrically arranged around a
tall pyramidal centerpiece or epergne piled with
fruits, nuts, and candied flower petals. Appearances
meant more than taste: an unimaginative display
would add no feathers to the hostess' cap while an
extravagantly fanciful setting would be admired and
talked about for years to come.

The fruit pyramid, a decorating staple since at

Photo courtesy of Colonial Williamsburg Foundation

least the sixteenth century, could be found in one form or another at the cor-
ners of most colonial dessert tables. A careful stacking of fruits, small cakes,

Centerpieces were meant to be eaten. Fruit, marzipan, jellies, nuts, and tiny cakes could be artfully arranged on a pyramid of glass salvers or in an epergne. The epergne, while more common on the tables of wealthy Englishmen than in the colonies, shows up on occasion in inventories of the Virginia aristocracy: Thomas Nelson of Yorktown, a signer of the Declaration of Independence, owned one. In the 1760s, William Byrd III of Westover had a silver epergne, perhaps something like this pagoda-style example that was made in London in 1762/3.

or candied sweetmeats into the shape of a cone or pyramid, this temporary table decoration was meant to be consumed. Large fruits like apples were usually balanced on top of one another, perhaps with a little sugar icing to keep them from tumbling off the table; smaller fruits like berries or cherries were poured into a metal cone-shaped mold and cemented together with sugar. Often topped with sprigs of holly, these edible pyramids went out of style in the early nineteenth century, except in Virginia where they persist today.

A lady's creativity and culinary skills were put to the supreme test by her centerpiece. The accomplished hostess tried to give an innovative twist to the rigidly proscribed etiquette of table decoration, creating a spectacle that would linger long in the memories of her guests. Hannah Glasse, an eighteenth-century Martha Stewart, warned her readers that talent was crucial to the success of the collation: "All this depends wholly on a little experience, and a good fancy to ornament in a pretty manner."[18] Ladies born to Virginia's aristocratic families labored alongside their cooks and servants to design miniature landscapes, complicated pastoral scenes with tiny figures, animals, flowers, and trees molded from sugar or marzipan, all edible. Mrs. Glasse's confectionery book—the leading one of its day—gives directions for many different centerpieces, among them this one:

> *"The above middle frame should be made either in three parts or five, all to join together, which may serve on different occasions on which suppose gravel walks, hedges, and variety of different things, as a little Chinese temple for the middle, or any other pretty ornament; which ornaments are to be bought at the confectioners, and will serve year after year; the top, bottom and sides are to be set out with such things as are to be got, or the season of the year will allow, as fruits, nuts of all kinds, creams, jellies, whip syllabubs, biscuits, etc. etc. and as many plates as you please, according to the size of the table."*[19]

Mrs. Glasse had other centerpiece recommendations. Place "A large dish with figures [figurines] and grass or moss about it, and flowers only for shew" in the center of an orderly arrangement of fruits, syllabubs, ice creams, and floating islands, she directed, or arrange "in the middle a high pyramid of one salver above another, the bottom one large, the next smaller, the top one less; these salvers are to be fill'd with all kinds of wet and dry sweet-meats in glass, baskets or little plates, colour'd jellies, creams, &c. biscuits, crisp'd almonds and little knicknacks, and bottles of flowers prettily intermix'd, the little top salver must have a large preserv'd Fruit in it." [20]

Not all centerpiece ornaments were edible. Porcelain figurines were the rage in the latter part of the eighteenth century, as were those made of

Photo courtesy of Colonial Williamsburg Foundation

A holiday dessert table garnished with holly uses a glass pyramid centerpiece to hold sweetmeats, jellies, and fresh fruits. According to custom, the top glass held an orange—a rare winter treat for Virginians who had to import such luxuries from the West Indies.

marble, wax, or plaster of Paris. They could be imported directly from London or purchased from Williamsburg shops. Milliner Sarah Pitt advertised in the *Virginia Gazette* that she had "Just imported in the *Industry*, Captain Lowes, from London . . . ornaments, and mottoes for desserts, of different sorts and figures." [21] Sets of figurines representing the seasons of the year, the four continents (Asia, Europe, America, Africa), and the mythology of ancient Greece and Rome predominated. Thomas Jefferson purchased a set of gods and goddesses in Paris at the request of his friend Abigail Adams.

> *"With respect to the figures I could only find three of those you named, matched in size," he wrote her playfully. "These were Minerva, Diana, and Apollo. I was obliged to add a fourth, unguided by your choice. They offered me a fine Venus, but I thought it out of taste to have two at table at the same time."* [22]

Often the centerpiece was arranged on a mirrored, raised platform called a "plateau." Guests who dined with President and Mrs. Washington at Christmas, 1795, admired the ornamental centerpiece with its plaster of Paris statuettes.

> *"In the middle of the table was placed a piece of table furniture about six feet long and two feet wide, rounded at the ends. It was either of wood gilded, or polished metal, raised about an inch with a silver rim round it like that round a tea board; in the centre was a pedestal of plaster of Paris with images upon it, and on each end figures; male and female, of the same. It was very elegant and used for ornament only. The dishes were placed all around, and there was an elegant variety of roast beef, veal, turkeys, ducks, fowls, hams, etc. puddings, jellies, oranges, apples, nuts, almonds, figs, raisins, and a variety of wines and punch. We took our leave at six, more than an hour after the candles were introduced. No lady but Mrs. Washington dined with us. We were Waited on by four or five men servants dressed in livery."* [23]

*W*assail *is a corruption of the Middle English* waes haeil *meaning "be whole" or healthy; the toast is usually translated, "to your health." There were as many versions of wassail as there were cooks to make it but it usually included ale, roasted apples, eggs, sugar, nutmeg, cloves, and ginger. Many of our punches and egg nogs are the culinary descendants of old wassail. There is no mention of wassail in colonial Virginia, although punch was common.*

Decorations

Even though no written sources describing colonial Virginia Christmas decorations have been discovered, historians have concluded that the usual English traditions continued in the colonies. Virginians considered themselves Englishmen in every sense of the word, clinging fast to their Old World traditions while trying just as hard to keep up with the latest London fashions. Hugh Jones, professor at the College of William and Mary and chaplain to the General Assembly, probably said it best. "The Habits, Life, Customs, Computations, &c. of the Virginians are much the same as about London, which they esteem their Home." [24] Reinforcing this conclusion are several nineteenth-century accounts that refer to indoor Christmas decorations as ancient custom.

We may reasonably assume that Englishmen living in Virginia decorated in much the same way as did Englishmen living in England, making proper allowance for the difference in native plant material. Virginia's holly, pine, and mistletoe resembled their English counterparts. Colonists soon included native American evergreens in the holiday decorating, plants such as magnolia, ground pine, and mountain laurel.

Evidence of eighteenth-century decorating has to be sought in pictorial representations, such as prints and paintings, and in prevailing English practices of that time. For example, holly, with its bright crimson berries, is pictured in many English prints of the eighteenth century, arranged in pretty vases, stuffed into crude pots, or stuck between the muntins and the window panes.

"From every hedge is plucked by eager hands
The holly-branch with prickly leaves replete,
And fraught with berries of a crimson hue;
Which torn asunder from its parent trunk,
Is straightway taken to the neighboring towns;
Where windows, mantels, candlesticks, and shelves,
Quarts, pints, decanters, pipkins, basins, jugs,
And other articles of household-ware,
The verdant garb confess." [25]

Photo courtesy of Colonial Williamsburg Foundation   Photo courtesy of Henry Francis duPont Winterthur Museum

These two English prints show various ways to decorate with holly and mistletoe during the eighteenth century.
In the tavern scene, a large bunch of mistletoe hangs from the ceiling beams and holly sprigs sprout from each
windowpane. In the kitchen, a sooty-faced chimney sweep spies the mistletoe and seizes his chance to give Betty,
the serving maid, a Christmas box or gift. All around the room, Betty has stuck holly and greens into pot lids
and other makeshift vases. (Detail from "English Alehouse," n.d.; "The Young Sweep gives Betty her Christmas
Box," London, circa 1780)

Judging from sources like these, it seems safest to say that Virginia colonists decorated for Christmas a little, a lot, or not at all, according to individual whim. Period prints show that the decorating impulse did not stop at
homes and churches—taverns and kitchens (in Virginia, a kitchen was a
small building separate from the main house) received their share as well. It
is likely that bouquets of winter greenery sat on tables and mantels in
bedchambers and parlours, that mistletoe hung from ceiling beams and
rafters, that dining and dessert tables were festively garnished, that sprigs of
holly were wedged between the wooden muntins of the window panes, and
that clusters of greenery adorned picture frames and mirrors. But outdoor
decorations of any kind, such as wreaths on the doors or candles in the windows, were unknown.

While Virginia's many rivers and ports permitted the colonists to import
some produce out of season, fresh fruit was far too costly to be wasted as

outdoor decoration, as we do today. Pineapples, oranges, limes, and lemons were imported by the barrel from British colonies in the tropical West Indies; apples and cranberries came from the northern American colonies. Expensive and rare, fresh fruit was treasured, especially during the winter months, and it would have occurred to no one in the eighteenth century to tack a fruited wreath onto his front door as decoration.

Church

The religious aspect of Christmas held its own against the flurry of holiday entertainments. Most people who lived within riding distance of a church attended service on Christmas Day, weather permitting; others said their prayers at home and read from the Bible or a book of published sermons. William Byrd II recorded his activities at Westover plantation on Christmas Day, 1740.

> *"I rose about 6, read Hebrew and Greek. I prayed and had coffee. I danced. The weather was very cold and cloudy, the wind north and threatened more snow. Nobody went to church except my son because of the cold. I put myself in order. After church came two playfellows for my son, young Stith and Hardyman. I ate roast turkey. After dinner we talked and I danced. I talked with my people [slaves] and prayed."* [26]

Virginia's established, or official, church was Anglican. While parish ministers differed as to the number of times per year they administered Holy Communion—three to nine was the range— Christmas Day was always one of those times.

Christmas decorations had been a common sight inside English and colonial churches since the early Middle Ages. An old fifteenth-century carol sings, "Holly and Ivy, Box and Bay, Put in the Church on

At the simple Anglican church at Westover plantation, the Byrd family would attend Christmas services with guests and neighbors.

Photo courtesy of Colonial Williamsburg Foundation

Christmas day." [27] The holiday was seen as an excuse to sweep out the cobwebs and carry in the cut greens. Garlands of holly, ivy, and mountain laurel often decorated the altars, encircled pillars, or wove their way through gallery railings, freshening the sanctuary with their woodsy scent. Peter Kalm, a Swedish botanist who visited Philadelphia at Christmas, 1749, took note of the custom. "Pews and altar were decorated with branches of mountain laurel, whose leaves are green in winter time. . ." [28] (An interesting aside: Kalm was a favorite pupil of Carolus Linnaeus who named the mountain laurel *Kalmia latifolia* for him.)

> "*I* had the pleasure to wait on Mrs Carter to Church She rode in the Chariot & Miss Prissy and Nancy; Mr Carter chose to stay at Home - The Sacrament was to have been administered but there was so few people that he thought it improper, and put it off til Sunday fortnight. He preach'd from Isaiah 9.6 For unto us a child is Born &c. his Sermon was fifteen Minutes long! very fashionable."
>
> (Fithian, Sunday Dec. 26, 1774)

Sometimes, it seems, people got a bit carried away in their church decorations. One London wit poked fun at decorations run riot in this satirical letter, published in 1712.

> "*I* am a young Woman, and have my Fortune to make; for which Reason I come constantly to Church to hear divine Service and make Conquests: But one great Hindrance in this my Design, is, that our Clerk, who was once a Gardener, has this Christmas so over deckt the Church with Greens, that he has quite spoilt my Prospect. . . The Church, as it is now equipt, looks more like a Green-house than a Place of Worship: The middle Isle is a very pretty shady Walk, and the Pews look like so many Arbours on each Side of it. The Pulpit it self has such Clusters of Ivy, Holly, and Rosemary about it," that the young miss could not see well enough to flirt with the gentleman sitting barely three pews away. Unless the excessive greenery was removed, she laments, she would have "little else to do there but say my Prayers." [29]

But having a church nearby did not guarantee a Christmas service. There was no Anglican bishop in Virginia—no one who could ordain new ministers—and this meant that all who served the church must come from England or travel to England from the colonies to be ordained. Such hardship led, quite predictably, to a shortage of ministers.

> *"I lament more and more every Sunday that we have no public place of worship to go to,"* wrote a young London merchant who was visiting a cousin in Tappahannock. *"There is a church to be sure, about three miles off, but unfortunately there happens to be no preacher. Being Christmas Day you miss it more than common. . ."* [30]

Barring Out the School Master

One centuries-old English custom that Virginia tutors heartily wished had remained in England was the "barring out" of the schoolmaster.

In order to force the schoolmaster to grant them a longer break in their studies at Christmas time, students would band together to barricade themselves inside the schoolhouse, often nailing shut windows and doors. As the teachers were always men, and the students were always boys (some not much younger than the schoolmaster himself), this romp had the potential to turn ugly. As it did in 1702. The Rev.

Francis Louis Michel, a Swiss national, toured the Virginia colony at the beginning of the eighteenth century, recording his observations with words and drawings. His sketch of the College of William and Mary in 1702 shows how the building looked during the barring out, a scandal that spilled over into a long-standing feud between Governor Francis Nicholson and College President James Blair, igniting a bitter lawsuit that ended only when the governor was transferred.

James Blair, founder and first president of the newly chartered College of William and Mary in Williamsburg, tells the story.

> *"About a fortnight before Christmas 1702 while I lodged in the College, I heard the School boys about 12 o'clock at night, a driving of great nails, to fasten & barracade the doors of the Grammar School. . . I made haste to get up & with the assistance of 2 servant men, I had in the College, I had almost forced open one of the doors before they sufficiently secured it, but while I was breaking in, they presently fired off 3 or 4 Pistols & hurt one of my servants in the eye with the wadd as I suppose of one of the Pistols, while I press'd forward, some of the Boys, having a great kindness for me, call'd out, `for God's sake sir don't offer to come in, for we have shot, & shall certainly fire at any one that first enters.'* [31]

Christmas "barring outs" had been an annual event at William and Mary since its founding and the event usually enjoyed the tacit connivance of the schoolmasters. In past years, President Blair had even joined in the fun—after the "barring out" negotiations had been concluded and the student holiday determined, there were some unspecified "entertainments" that had been paid for by the governor himself.

> *"[W]hen I was a Scholar [in 1699], We Shutt the Doors against our Masters at which time his Excellcy [the governor] gave us money to buy Victuals & Drink & after we had obtained leave to be dismist & had opened the School Doors, Mr. Blair himself together with Sevll of his Relations participated of the entertainmt which we had provided with the money aforesaid."* [32]

Soon "their majesties' royall colledge" started granting students a set holiday from December 16 until the first Monday after Epiphany (or Twelfth Day, January 6). For the boys in the Grammar School, the Indian School, and the College, "barring out" was over forever.

But far more boys (and sometimes even girls) were educated at home by private tutors than attended the College or were sent back "home" to English schools. Private tutors gave holidays at their own discretion. Those who granted an insufficient number of days could find themselves "barred out."

"Mr. Goodlet [a tutor at the Fauntleroy plantation] was barr'd out of his School last Monday by his Scholars, for the Christmas Holidays, which are to continue til twelf-day;" noted a fellow tutor at Nomini Hall plantation. With understandable relief, he continued, "But my Scholars are of a more quiet nature, and have consented to have four or five Days now, and to have their full Holiday in May next, when I propose by the permission of Providence to go Home." [33]

Christmas Gifts

Gift-giving was not a big part of a colonial Virginia Christmas. The English Christmas box tradition held sway in Virginia but it bore little resemblance to the wrapped presents we have associated with the holiday since Victorian times.

Tradesmen's apprentices and servants in medieval England looked forward to the Christmas box custom when, throughout the holiday season—indeed, sometimes well into the new year—customers were expected to tip these underlings by dropping a coin or two into a rounded clay vessel, the ancestor of our piggy bank. After the holidays, the cheap clay box was broken and the money spent, usually on strong drink. The custom traces its origins to imperial Rome, where masters gave servants coins on festival days. It further evolved into Boxing Day, the holiday celebrated in England and Canada on December 26 with the exchange of gifts.

For colonial Virginians, however, a Christmas box came to mean the tip or

Photo courtesy of Colonial Williamsburg Foundation

The English Christmas box is the precursor to the piggy bank. In England, a Christmas box referred both to the clay container and to the present of money that went in it. An apprentice might receive a few coins as a Christmas box and put them in his Christmas box. In colonial Virginia, the custom evolved differently: Christmas box meant only the actual gift, whether this was a tip given by members of the gentry to apprentices, servants, or slaves, or a small present given by fathers to their children.

gift *itself* rather than the clay box that held it. Fithian noted the curious local custom in his diary. On Christmas Day he gave a Christmas box of several shillings to a few of the Carter house slaves:

> *"Nelson the Boy who makes my Fire, blacks my shoes, does errands &c. was early in my Room, drest only in his shirt and Breeches! He made me a vast fire, blacked my shoes, set my Room in order, and wish'd me a joyful Christmas, for which I gave him half a Bit. - Soon after he left the Room, and before I was Drest, the Fellow who makes the Fire in our School Rooms, drest very neatly in green, but almost drunk, entered my chamber with three or four profound Bows,& made me the same salutation; I gave him a Bit, and dismissed him as soon as possible. - Soon after my Cloths and Linen were sent in with a message for a Christmas Box, as they call it; I sent the poor Slave a Bit, & many thanks. I was obliged for want of small change, to put off for some days the Barber who shaves & dresses me. - I gave Tom the Coachman . . . two Bits . . . I gave to Dennis the Boy who waits at Table half a Bit — So that the sum of my Donations to the Servants, for this Christmas appears to be five Bits, a Bit is a pisterene bisected or an English sixpence, & passes here for seven pence Halfpenny."* [34]

None of these people put their money in a clay box—that tradition seems to have been confined to England where it continued until the early part of the twentieth century—yet everyone called the tip itself a "Christmas box."

In the Christmas Day entry of one of his notebooks, Thomas Jefferson wrote, "gave Christmas gifts" to the amount of 48 shillings. [35] The money may have gone for year-end tips to servants and slaves. But these were the years when the old Virginia Christmas box tradition started to include children, so it is possible that part of the 48 shillings was given to Jefferson's daughters. A youngster's gift was less likely to be money than it was a book, candy, or some personal item. Williamsburg storekeepers advertised in the *Virginia Gazette* that they stocked merchandise—usually books with a religious or moral purpose—intended as a Christmas box for children. More likely than not, the gift came at New Year's instead of Christmas.

> *"Lately Published, (being very proper for a New-Year's Gift to Children,)*
> *THE Church Catechism Explain'd; by Way of Question and Answer; and*

Symmetry, a hallmark of Georgian style, governed the decorative arts. Whether the subject was architecture, interior design, landscaping, or food presentation, symmetrical designs predominated. Occasionally gardens and dining tables overlapped: centerpieces with pathways, shrubbery, statuary, mirror lakes, and architectural embellishments were the result. In 1769, Virginia's popular royal governor, Norborne Berkeley, Baron de Botetourt, gave a ball and dazzled his Williamsburg guests with a centerpiece scene that featured a garden with a miniature Chinese temple.

Photos courtesy of Colonial Williamsburg Foundation

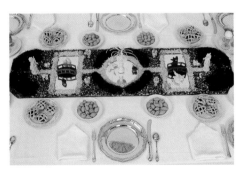 

Figurines on the table were all the rage in the late colonial period. Elaborate scenes, like this fountain spectacle, could incorporate in their design small animals or figures made of porcelain, marble, edible marzipan, or plaster of Paris. Housewives who could not afford store-bought figurines could purchase copper molds and make their own from wax or colored sugar.

Photos courtesy of Colonial Williamsburg Foundation

On an elaborately set table, late-ripening lady apples in a silver epergne and pyramids of little cakes give the scene a festive air.

The modest table setting makes use of two glass salvers and some simple figurines for an elegant centerpiece.

In colonial times, the presentation of the dish was often more important than its taste. These holiday desserts, based on eighteenth-century recipes, are arranged and decorated in eighteenth-century style. At center, the simulated snow mound is garnished with sprigs of rosemary and marzipan strawberries.

In colonial Virginia, buildings were illuminated with candles in the windows on occasions of public celebration. Williamsburg may have looked something like this when, a few days before Christmas, 1769, the Capitol was illuminated for "a ball and elegant entertainment" given by "the Gentlemen of the Hon. the House of Burgesses to his Excellency the Governour, his Majesty's Council, and the Gentlemen and Ladies of this city."

Photos courtesy of Colonial Williamsburg Foundation

Today, Virginia's historic churches decorate for Christmas by borrowing from four centuries of tradition. Bruton Parish Church in Williamsburg continues the ancient English custom known as "the sticking of the Church with greens" by decorating with garlands of pine roping. The Christmas Eve poinsettias are Victorian era embellishments, and the fruited wreaths come from the twentieth century.

confirm'd by Scripture Proofs: Divided into Five Parts, and 12 Sections. . .
Printed, and Sold by William Parks. Price stitch'd 10d. bound 15d." [36]

By the middle of the eighteenth century, a few publishers were turning out children's books specifically intended as holiday gifts: among them *Nurse Truelove's Christmas-Box, Nurse Truelove's New-Year's Gift,* and other titles for Twelfth Day, Easter, Valentine's Day, and Whitsuntide. Published annually, they contained a selection of short stories plus a little poetry. This "gift" series, along with other books like *Robinson Crusoe,* Aesop's Fables, the *History of England,* poetry, Bibles, and prayer books, give a good idea of the sort of holiday present an upper class child might receive. [37]

Still, the gift-giving was going in one direction only— the same direction it had been going since Roman times— from master to servant, adult to child, superior to inferior. It wasn't until early in the nineteenth century that the custom of exchanging gifts between friends and family members took hold and Christmas presents replaced Christmas boxes. [38]

Photo courtesy of Colonial Williamsburg Foundation

Late in the eighteenth century, when the Christmas box custom spread to children, the nature of the gift changed from coins to small presents, more often than not, books with a religious or moral theme.

Twelfth Night

The Twelve Days of Christmas began with December 25 and ended on January 6, appropriately called Twelfth Night. Officially, this marked the end of the Christmas season, although there were some zealots who celebrated right through to February. On the Anglican church calendar, January 6 was Epiphany, the celebration of the visit of the Magi, or Three Wise Men. In some Virginia homes Twelfth Night was the most festive occasion of the season.

*"It seems," wrote Cresswell, our English spy travelling through north-
ern Virginia shortly before the Revolution, "this is one of their annual Balls
supported in the following manner: A large rich cake is provided and cut
into small pieces and handed round to the company, who at the same time
draws a ticket out of a Hat with something merry wrote on it. He that
draws the King has the Honor of treating the company with a Ball the next
year, which generally costs him Six or Seven Pounds. The Lady that draws
the Queen has the trouble of making the Cake. Here was about 37 ladies
dressed and powdered to the life, some of them very handsome and as much
vanity as is necessary. All of them fond of dancing, but I do not think they
perform it with the greatest elegance. Betwixt the Country dances they have
what I call everlasting jigs. A couple gets up and begins to dance a jig (to
some Negro tune) others comes and cuts them out, and these dances always
last as long as the Fiddler can play. This is sociable, but I think it looks
more like a Bacchanalian dance than one in a polite assembly. Old Women,
Young Wives with young children in the lap, widows, maids and girls come
promiscuously to these assemblies which generally continue till morning. A
cold supper, Punch, Wines, Coffee and Chocolate, but no Tea. This is a
forbidden herb [due to the colonial boycott of tea]."* [39]

THE VILLAGE ASSEMBLY

Photo courtesy of Colonial Williamsburg Foundation
*"Dancing is the chief diversion here," wrote John Kello of Hampton to a London friend in 1755.
("The Village Assembly," England, 1776)*

Landon Carter of Sabine Hall, situated in Virginia's Northern Neck, usually marked Twelfth Night with a three-day feast.

> *"From the 1st day of this month till this day we have had prodigious fine weather indeed, so that I have enjoyed my three days' festival to-wit: The 10, 11 and 12, with great cheerfulness to everybody; in all about 60 people."* [40]

Nor was Landon Carter the only one in his neighborhood celebrating Twelfth Night. "Captn. Beale had invited this family yesterday to a dinner and a twelfth cake," he wrote in 1770. [41]

Twelfth Night seems not to have been celebrated in colonies north of Virginia. Abigail Adams, born and raised in Massachusetts, had never heard of it.

Weddings

The Christmas season was a favorite time for weddings, since so many were gathered together and in a celebratory frame of mind. Typically, an Anglican minister performed the brief ceremony at the bride's home as relatives and guests looked on. George Washington wed Martha Dandridge Custis during the Christmas holidays in 1759 at White House, Martha's home in New Kent County. Thomas Jefferson married the widow Martha Wayles Skelton at The Forest, the Wayles family home in Charles City County, on New Year's Day, 1772. Unfortunately, no description of either of these weddings has

Photo courtesy of Wilton House Museum

come down to the present, but it was typical for marriage ceremonies to be followed with singing, dancing, music, and an elegant supper.

One detailed account of a Williamsburg wedding does survive. William Wirt, the noted writer and lawyer who would soon gain fame as the prosecutor of Aaron Burr and later as attorney general of the United States, attended a winter wedding. He paints a vivid picture of the event for his wife who could not come.

"It was past eleven when the sanctum sanctorum of the supper-room was thrown open . . . and it was near twelve when it came to my turn to see the show. And a very superb one it was I assure you. The tree in the centre cake was more simply elegant than any thing of the kind I remember to have seen. It was near four feet high: the cake itself, the pedestal, had a rich—very rich—fringe of white paper surrounding it: the leaves, baskets, garlands, &c., &c., were all very naturally done in white paper, not touched with the pencil, and the baskets were rarely ornamented with silver spangles. At the ends of the tables were two lofty pyramids of jellies, syllabubs, ice-creams, &c.,—the which pyramids were connected with the tree in the cen-

Photo courtesy of Wilton House Museum

At Wilton House Museum in Richmond, staff re-created a winter wedding scene from William Wirt's detailed description.

tre cake by pure white paper chains, very prettily cut, hanging in light and delicate festoons, and ornamented with paper bow-knots. Between the centre cake and each pyramid was another large cake made for use: then there was a profusion of meats, cheese-cakes, fruits, etc., etc." [42]

Christmastime for Slaves and Servants

No one looked forward to Christmas as much as slaves and indentured servants. It was the one time of the year they could expect a few days off from work, some good food, and enough alcohol to drown their troubles. Most plantation owners followed the custom of granting several days leisure to their "people" and, in the old English tradition of feasting one's neighbors "both great and small," doled out rations of meat and strong spirits to all.

Ironically, house servants, the much envied upper crust of the serving class, would not likely have received much of a break at Christmas. In fact, they probably worked harder during the season to prepare the holiday meals and to care for guests and extra horses, but they may have been compensated with extra gifts or tips.

Photo courtesy of the Abby Aldrich Rockefeller Folk Art Museum, Williamsburg, VA

"The Old Plantation," artist unidentified, possibly 1790-1800

Because most indentured servants and slaves were illiterate, few accounts survive describing their lives from their own points of view. Plantation owners and visitors to Virginia occasionally noted that servants and slaves took the opportunity to organize their own worship services and to celebrate the season with song and dance, much like their masters. On Christmas Day, Fithian noted that "Guns are fired this Evening in the Neighbourhood, and the Negroes seem to be inspired with new Life." [43] Reverend John Wright, a Presbyterian minister in Cumberland County, Virginia, gave us this look at Christmas in the slave quarters shortly before the Revolutionary War.

> *"My landlord tells me, when he waited on the Colonel at his country-seat two or three days, they heard the Slaves at worship in the lodge, singing Psalms and Hymns in the evening, and again in the morning, long before the break of day. The are excellent singers, and long to get some of Dr. Watt's Psalms and Hymns, which I encourage them to hope for."* (Dr. Isaac Watts was an English Congregationalist minister whose hymn book was a favorite among Virginians, white and black. His best known hymn today is probably "Joy to the World.") [44]

By the end of the colonial period, Christmas had taken on greater role in the life of most Virginia slaves. In spite of the efforts of the planter aristocracy to limit "dissenters" (anyone who differed in religious opinion from the established Anglican church, such as Baptists, Methodists, and Quakers), the Great Awakening of the mid-eighteenth century saw Virginia flooded with evangelical preaching. These itinerants brought with them a more emotional, easy-to-understand theology that appealed primarily to Virginia's poor and, not surprisingly, to those in bondage. Williamsburg's first Baptist congregation, established in the 1780s on Nassau Street, consisted of slaves and free blacks who embraced this emotional style of preaching.

As Christianity became increasingly important in the slaves' lives, so did Christmas. The old one-day holiday stretched into several days and finally a week or longer. Greater freedoms were allowed. At the dawn of the nineteenth century, a set of Christmas customs unknown to earlier slaves had taken effect across the South.

A Frontier Virginia Christmas

Geography caused an unusual settlement pattern in the western part of Virginia. Instead of the east-to-west movement that characterizes American expansion, the lush land in the Valley of Virginia was settled along the line of least resistance, from north to south. Thus it was first settled not by Englishmen from the east but by Germans and Scotch-Irish moving south from Pennsylvania.

Because of the great ethnic and religious variation in early western Virginia, there was no uniform celebration of Christmas. On much of the Virginia frontier, Christmas was hardly noticed. One reason was surely the rough lifestyle which, understandably, was both simpler and more dangerous than life in the Tidewater region. But the real reason was the people. Settlers in Virginia's remote wild west were not, by and large, the sort of Protestants who "kept Christmas."

Early in the eighteenth century, the first major wave of Scotch-Irish and German settlers immigrated to the middle colonies, entering through the port of Philadelphia and moving on to the rich farmland on the western Pennsylvania frontier. Many turned south, following the Shenandoah River, coming into Virginia around Harper's Ferry and moving south into the Valley of Virginia.

Photo courtesy of Museum of American Frontier Culture

At the Virginia Museum of American Frontier Culture, a farm built in 1850 shows elements of the region's German, English, and Scotch-Irish traditions.

Although, strictly speaking, Virginia law classified these settlers as "dissenters" and forbade their practicing a religion that competed with the established Anglican church, authorities in Williamsburg knew when to allow exceptions to the rule—especially when it put *other* people between themselves and the Indians. By the 1730s, Virginia burgesses were actually encouraging Scotch-Irish Presbyterians and others who did not happen to share the Anglican fondness for Christmas to settle the frontier as a buffer against the French and Indians.

The largest immigrant group to settle the Virginia frontier was loosely known as "the Germans" (erroneously referred to on occasion as "Dutch," a corruption of the word "Deutsch" and not an identification with Holland). These people were natives of various German-speaking regions, primarily Switzerland, the Palatinate and Bavaria (southern Germany), and Bohemia and Moravia (Czech Republic). They farmed the rich Valley soil and traded for furs and deerskin with the Indians. The first of their number settled the Valley during the 1720s and 30s in the area south of Winchester, Virginia, in today's Page, Shenandoah, and Frederick counties. In matters of faith, most were Lutheran or Mennonite. Lutherans who retained some of the Catholic Church year in their worship observed Christmas Day in church and at home; Mennonites did not observe Christmas at all. [45]

Nicholas Cresswell, wishing he were home in England instead of in Virginia on December 25, 1776, grumbled in his journal about the lack of celebration in the area of Frederick County. "Christmas Day, but very little observed in this country, except it is amongst the Dutch [probably Lutheran Germans]." Over the next few days he continued to complain about his reduced circumstances and his inability to return to his native land. New Year's Day was a little pleasanter for him, as he "Spent the day very happily at Mr. Gibbs with a few of his friends, dancing and making ourselves merry as Whiskey, Toddy and good company will afford."[46] New Year's Day could be celebrated by all.

A little further south in Staunton, tutor Philip Fithian, now a missionary to a flock of Scotch-Irish Presbyterians and still keeping his journal, found much the same thing. It was a Christmas much different from his last one on the Carter plantation. For the inhabitants of this part of the colony, Christmas was another work day. Stores and schools were open. Churches were closed. Business continued as usual. Nonetheless, the famous Virginia hospitality had not diminished and the frontier folk did eat well, Christmas or not.

> *"Christmas Morning. - Not a Gun is heard - Not a Shout - No company*
> *or Cabal assembled - To Day is like other Days every Way calm & temperate*
> *- People go about their daily Business with the same Readiness, & apply*

themselves to it with the same Industry, as they used - The Air of Virginia seems to inspire all the Inhabitants with Hospitality - It has long been a Characteristic of the lower Counties - I am sure these Western ones deserve it - Everything they possess is as free to a Stranger as the Water or the Air... Since I left Stephensburg I have seen no Coffee, Chocolate - Tea is out of the Question; it is almost Treason against the Country to mention it, much more to drink it. . . But in the Place of these plenty of rich Milk in large Basins, & Noggins; to which you may put your Mouth, & drink without Order or Measure - Large Platters covered with Meat of many Sorts; Beef; Venison; Pork; - & with these Potatoes, Turnips, Cabbage, & Apples beyond your Asking - A low Bench for a Table you will have covered with such Provisions three Times every Day." [47]

If Fithian had been in the valley areas inhabited by Lutheran Germans, he would have recognized the celebration as similar to that of Tidewater Virginia. These German Virginians celebrated Christmas by "playing, drinking and feasting." They attended church, ate and drank excessively, fired Christmas guns, and shot in the New Year much like their English counterparts to the east. [48] Presbyterian minister David McClure visited some of these settlements in 1773 and wrote in his diary, "Rode 7 miles to Mr. Stevensons's and preached. The hearers mostly Virginians. . . Several present, appeared almost intoxicated. Christmas and New Year holly days, are seasons of wild mirth and disorder here." [49]

VIRGINIA ALMANACK FOR THE YEAR OF OUR LORD GOD 1764

"Christmas draws near, take Care to get The Plate and Dishes, Pot and Spit; But still take Care, when all is done, You something have to put thereon."

*Y*oung St. George Tucker came to Virginia from Bermuda in 1771 to attend the College of William and Mary. Christmas customs are mentioned in some of his surviving family letters:

"Your Holydays I suppose you will spend with your Relations in Norfolk - & as you are fond of dancing, I dare say, you will pass your Christmas merrily."
December 8, 1771

"A merry Christmas to you. My dearest St. George, - & that every New Year may bring an Addition of Happiness to you."
December 25, 1772

"I hope you have spent the Christmas chearfully & merrily - May you live to see many Returns of this Season of common Festivity & may each succeeding one be happier than the last! . . . Ps I had almost forgot to tell you that my Fanny begs your Acceptance of a pair of silk Stockings for a Christmas Box."
January 4, 1773

"Governor Bruere [of Bermuda] presents his Compliments to Mr St George Tucker by Capt Brigs and Wishess Mr Tucker many, many happy Years. hath sent Him a bunch of Bananas supposing it may be a rarity especially at this time of the Year."
January 4, 1773

End Notes

1. Wright, Louis B., ed., <u>History and Present State of Virginia</u>, pp. 312-13.
2. Cresswell, Nicholas, <u>Journal of Nicholas Cresswell</u>, pp. 271-72.
3. "Christmas," <u>London Magazine</u>, 1746.
4. Goodwin, Mary R. M., "Christmas in Colonial Virginia," p. 16.
5. Farish, Hunter D., ed. <u>The Journal and Letters of Philip Vickers Fithian</u>, p. 34.
6. Carson, Jane, <u>Colonial Virginians at Play</u>, p. 139. Burnaby visited the colony in 1759-60.
7. <u>Ibid.</u>, p. 140.
8. Mordecai, Samuel, <u>Richmond in By-Gone Days</u>, pp. 355-56.
9. Goodwin, "Christmas in Colonial Virginia," p. xvii.
10. Farish, Hunter D., ed. <u>The Journal and Letters of Philip Vickers Fithian</u>, p. 39.
11. <u>Ibid.</u>, p. 34.
12. The authors are indebted to Jane Carson's <u>Colonial Virginians at Play</u> for information on games, activities, and other entertainments of the colonial period.
13. Farish, Hunter D., ed. <u>The Journal and Letters of Philip Vickers Fithian</u>, p. 37.
14. DeSimone, David, "Another Look at Christmas in the Eighteenth Century," <u>Interpreter</u> (Winter 1995-96), p. 7.
15. This poem, dating to 1577, is found in Thomas Tusser, <u>Five Hundred Pointes of Good Husbandrie</u>, p. 225.
16. The quote from Elizabeth Raffald's 1775 book, <u>The Experienced English Housekeeper</u>, is found in Wendy Howell, "Setting a Fine Table," <u>Interpreter</u> (Winter 1996-97). The authors are indebted to Howell and also to Louise Belden, <u>The Festive Tradition: Table Decoration and Desserts in America, 1650-1900</u>, to Mary Goodwin, "Christmas in Colonial Virginia," and to Kathryn Arnold for their information on table settings, food, and decoration.
17. This December verse from a 1714 almanac is found in Nissembaum's <u>The Battle for Christmas</u>, p. 23.
18. Glasse, Hannah, <u>The Complete Confectioner</u>, p. 255.
19. <u>Ibid.</u>, p. 255.
20. <u>Ibid.</u>, pp. 254 and 263.
21. <u>Virginia Gazette</u>, December 14, 1769.
22. Ford, Paul Leicester, <u>The Writings of Thomas Jefferson</u>, p. 99.
23. Goodwin, Mary, "Christmas in Colonial Virginia," p. xxxix.
24. Jones, Hugh, <u>The Present State of Virginia</u>, p. 43.
25. Warren, Nathan B., <u>The Christmas Book: Christmas in the Olden Time</u>, p. 13.

26. Goodwin, Mary, "Christmas in Colonial Virginia," p. vii.

27. Tille, Alexander, Yule and Christmas: Their Place in the Germanic Year, p. 106.

28. DeSimone, David, "Another Look at Christmas in the Eighteenth Century," Interpreter (Winter 1995-96), p. 6.

29. Bond, Donald, ed., The Spectator, vol. II, p. 600.

30. Entry in Robert Hunter, Jr.'s diary of December 25, 1785, found in Mary Goodwin, "Christmas in Colonial Virginia," p. xxxvii.

31. Goodwin, Mary, "Historical Notes: The College of William and Mary," pp. 90-91.

32. Ibid., pp. 89-101, and J. E. Morpurgo, Their Majesties' Royall Colledge, pp. 54-56.

33. Farish, Hunter Dickinson, ed. The Journal of Philip Vickers Fithian, p. 34.

34. Ibid., pp. 39-40.

35. From Jefferson's 1779 account book, in Harold Gill, "Christmas in Colonial Virginia," Colonial Williamsburg Journal (October-November, 1999), p. 12.

36. Virginia Gazette, February 25, 1768.

37. The authors are indebted to Pat Gibbs, historian at Colonial Williamsburg, for her information on children's literature. These titles and others found in the Virginia Gazette, February 25, 1768.

38. Noel Hume, Ivor, "'Twas the Day After Christmas," Colonial Williamsburg Journal, pp. 54-57; and David DeSimone, "The Christmas Box Tradition," Interpreter, p. 1.

39. Cresswell, Nicholas, Journal of Nicholas Cresswell, pp. 52-53.

40. Carter's diary of 1771 in Jane Carson, Colonial Virginians at Play, p. 5.

41. Landon Carter's diary January 7, 1770, quoted in Wendy Howell, "Setting a Fine Table: the Christmas Season," Interpreter, p. 7.

42. Carson, Jane, Colonial Virginians at Play, p. 8.

43. Farish, Hunter D., ed. The Journal and Letters of Philip Vickers Fithian, p. 39.

44. DeSimone, David, "Another Look at Christmas in the Eighteenth Century," Interpreter, p. 7.

45. Wust, Klaus, The Virginia Germans, p. 37.

46. Goodwin, Mary, "Christmas in Colonial Virginia," p. xxxiv.

47. Fithian's journal of December 25, 1775, in David DeSimone, "Christmas in Revolutionary Times," Interpreter, p. 2.

48. Wust, Klaus, The Virginia Germans, p. 175.

49. McClure's diary in Alfred L. Shoemaker, Christmas in Pennsylvania, p. 6.

Chapter Three

"Children Danced and Shouted"

The Origin of the American Christmas

Today's Christmas season is crammed as full as St. Nick's pack with traditions old and new. Some of the customs Americans hold dear date to the colonial period when the country's fortunes were linked tightly to the English motherland; a few can claim pagan origins even more ancient. But many of our most treasured traditions, like the Christmas tree and Santa Claus, are gifts from our German and Dutch heritage, introduced during the nineteenth century. Pieced together, old with new, they form a patchwork quilt of holiday customs that became the American Christmas.

The most significant change came about during the early eighteen-hundreds. In a matter of a couple decades, the holiday that had for centuries been synonymous with adult revelry was stripped of its rowdier elements and transformed into a more peaceful, respectable, home-based celebration with the focus squarely on the children. This re-casting of Christmas as the calendar's premiere family event was led by Americans Washington Irving and Clement C. Moore and by Englishman Charles Dickens. Writing in the early part of the nineteenth century, Washington Irving created the first glimpse of a Christmas celebration that we would recognize today. It was he

The image of Queen Victoria and her family that popularized Christmas trees in England and America first appeared in a London magazine in 1848. Two years later (and again in 1860), Godey's Lady's Book, the most popular American women's magazine, published a slightly altered version.

who popularized St. Nicholas, patron saint of New Amsterdam, but it was left to Clement Moore in 1823 to write the definitive description of the "right jolly old elf" who flew through the sky with his reindeer to deliver presents to children "and a happy Christmas to all." A generation later and an ocean away, Charles Dickens added the English element with his wildly popular story, "A Christmas Carol."

By the middle of the nineteenth century, all the elements of today's Christmas were firmly in place. Tabletop Christmas trees decorated with sweets and small toys for the children were gaining in popularity on both sides of the sea, thanks to Her Majesty Queen Victoria. Pictures of the Christmas trees that Prince Albert set up each year for the royal children made the rounds of the ladies magazines, lending immense prestige to the custom. Santa Claus and his wondrous reindeer had been solidly established in the hearts and minds of American children. The first Christmas card—it was English—appeared in 1843. "A Merry Christmas and a Happy New Year to You," it read. The idea flew across the Atlantic and soon Americans too were exchanging printed cards with friends and relations.

As might be expected, Virginians embraced the "new" Christmas traditions with enthusiasm, adding them to existing customs without subtracting anything. In 1849 Virginia became the fifth state to recognize Christmas as a legal holiday, which meant that the courts and other state offices would close. This was nothing new—most farmers and businessmen in the eastern part of Virginia had been taking Christmas Day off for over two hundred years and by long custom the royal governor had adjourned the House of Burgesses for the holidays—but now it was official. Slaves found their Christmas respite extended from one or two days to a week or more, depending upon their master's generosity. Schoolmasters gave their scholars a holiday without having to be "barred out" of the classroom. And scarcely a diary or journal fails to mention the weddings that were celebrated over the holiday season.

Still, not everyone in Virginia "kept Christmas." Like the Puritans in New England, the Scotch-Irish Presbyterians in the Valley of Virginia diligently ignored it. So did the Baptists, the Methodists, the Mennonites, the Brethren, and the Quakers who settled this farmer's paradise. Although they were not Puritans, they were intensely biblical and shared some of the Puritan attitudes about religion. For them, the day passed with churches closed and businesses open.

"They want to hear nothing of Christmas," wrote Rev. Henry Harbaugh with frustration when his preaching among the Scotch-Irish met with failure. "They spend the day working as on any other day. Their children grow up knowing nothing of brightly lit Christmas trees, nor Christmas presents. God have mercy on these Presbyterians—these pagans." [1]

Many in the North persisted in regarding Christmas as a southern holiday, as foreign to Northerners as snow was to the South. "In this country Christmas has never been fully observed, except in the South," stated one Pennsylvania newspaper shortly after the Civil War. "The self-righteous Puritans who settled New England thought it a sin to be glad . . . The Dutch settlers of New Amsterdam made New Year's day the great annual holiday of New Year. In Pennsylvania Christmas has always been honored; but it was never celebrated with an approach to old English heartiness except in the South." [2] The newspaper was right about one thing: Southerners were not content to merely *observe* Christmas. They celebrated.

Victorian Decorations

Victorian style provided the perfect backdrop for the new holiday customs. No one, before or since, has decorated like the Victorians, or with such abandon. Romantic, sentimental, and fussy, Victorians tolerated no blank wall, no uncluttered table top, no unpatterned surface. More was better. More than that, better still. Christmas was the pinnacle of decorating extravagance.

Household guides, women's magazines, letters, and period prints shed a bright light upon the nature of Christmas decorations during these years. Before the Civil War virtually all Christmas decorations and ornaments were home made. Mixing a pinch of imagination with a dollop of local plant material was still the best recipe for Christmas cheer.

Holly, cedar, arbor-vitae, yew, myrtle, boxwood, laurel, ivy, and pine were tied into garland ropes called "wreathing" and draped in festoons around the room, across entranceways, over mirrors and mantels, around pictures, and later, when gas lighting became available, suspended from gasoliers. Somehow this was all to be accomplished without placing plant material "upside down, as foliage must never be placed in a direction contrary to that of its growth." [3] Barrel hoops worked well as support for garlands or crinoline cane could be bent into hoops which, covered with evergreen, made fine round wreaths to hang on windows or around portraits. Star and shield shapes hung on the walls. Mistletoe kissing balls had become a holiday staple. More imaginative people twisted holly around chains of hanging lamps and suspended a small basket filled with mistletoe from it. Vases of cut greens decked the mantels of fireplaces even in the bedrooms.

Photo courtesy of Maymont Foundation

Flowers and evergreen garlands were staples of Victorian Christmas decoration. Maymont's Dooley mansion in Richmond is decorated according to styles of the 1890s.

"The old portraits extended all around the room and were decorated with wreaths of holly and cedar and a bright log fire cast a warm glow over everything. . . The lofty dining-room directly across the hall was also decorated in holly and cedar." [4]

The Victorians did not allow their love affair with flowers to be stymied by cold weather. In winter, dried flowers called "immortelles" were widely incorporated into boxwood arrangements. Potted plants had their places on floors and tabletops. Wherever camellias, chrysanthemums, primulas, and Christmas roses bloomed in winter, people made good use of their blossoms. Where no real flowers were available, colored paper, especially gilt, made bright flowers and ornaments for tabletop trees and wreathing. Not only were private homes and churches targets of the Christmas decorators, but schoolrooms and public halls as well. After the Civil War, poinsettias began appearing in the flower shops; by the turn of the twentieth century they had become the principle flower of the season, carried in Christmas weddings, used to decorate churches and homes, and given as gifts.

Not for nothing was holly called the "prince of evergreens." It was every-

Photo courtesy of Maymont Foundation

"In planning for Christmas festivities the question of table decoration is of real importance," begins the Ladies Home Journal of December 1893. "At either end of the table stand the candelabra, which for this occasion should have red candles and red shades. At each lady's place have a corsage bouquet of bright red flowers tied with red ribbon, and for the gentlemen boutonnieres of mistletoe. Have suspended over the table . . . red ribbons about an inch wide . . . and tie in a bow."

where, its prickly sprigs wedged into picture frames and clocks, twisted around the chains of chandeliers, arranged in vases, fastened to the tops of draperies, and stuck into holiday dishes as a garnish, even pinned into women's hair. A clever young lady might make up a pyramid of holly sprigs stuck into moss for the dining room table. Baskets of holly sprigs sat on tables, banks of holly boughs were arranged behind vases of holly on the fireplace mantel. Some of Virginia's earliest Christmas trees were holly. Alice West Allen, who was eleven years old when she attended a Christmas party in Richmond in 1864, recalled:

> *"A dear friend of my mother's found that we were to spend Christmas in the city, so she invited us to a Christmas tree given to President Davis' children. The tree was a lovely holly laden with homemade candles and dolls made out of hickory nuts and Canton flannel; then there were cotton and*

Canton flannel rabbits, dogs and cats, and numerous other presents all home-made, as was everything on the supper table—homemade coffee, tea, sugar, and everything. I have never seen anything that looked so pretty to me." [5]

Everything that could be decorated was decorated, at home and at church. Cordons of evergreens wrapped around pedestals, banisters, pillars, and columns. Mirrors, portraits, and windows were framed with wreathing. If an entrance hall had wainscotting, narrow borders of boxwood and ivy were rec-

Photo courtesy of Maymont Foundation

THE CHRISTMAS FLOWER

In 1825, The United States sent diplomat Joel Roberts Poinsett to Mexico City as our country's first official ambassador to the newly formed Mexican republic. During his four-year stay, Poinsett, who was also an accomplished amateur botanist, came across a beautiful native plant with bright red and green foliage. He sent specimens back to the States where they were raised and sold at select greenhouses. The plant became known in the United States as the poinsettia.

With their striking red and green coloration, it was probably inevitable that poinsettias would come to be associated with Christmas. However, it was not until after the Civil War that they began appearing in New York shops over the holidays. By the turn of the century, poinsettias had become the principle flower of the season. Each year over 60 million plants are sold. [6]

Contrary to persistent rumors, the poinsettia is not poisonous to animals or to humans. However, the plant is not a food and should be kept out of the reach of curious youngsters.

ommended. Festoons of evergreen hung from nails fixed close to the ceiling. Children strung garlands of popcorn, cranberries, holly berries, or holly leaves (ouch!), and made paper chains.

> *"The gathering of evergreens and mistletoe was the sign that Christmas had come," recalled Thomas Nelson Page, the Virginia novelist, historian, and lawyer who practically invented the "Old South." "There was the parlor and hall and dining room to be 'dressed,' and, above all, the old church. The last was the work of the neighborhood; all united in it, and it was one of the events of the year. Young men rode thirty and forty miles to 'help' dress that church. They did not go home again till after Christmas."* [7]

In the deep South, Spanish moss made an unusual sort of decoration. One Mississippi woman recalled that her "house was decorated with gray moss, holly and mistletoe and magnolia leaves were on the tablecloth." Virginians used green moss; just how they used it is not clear. One young lady from Warrenton wrote, "The parlor has been tastefully dressed by Bert, Vic and F. with running pine and holly bearing its red berries. Other ornaments made of moss decorate the walls." She may well have been describing something that household guides of the period were recommending: green moss or rice glued onto cardboard to spell out a holiday greeting or monogram. [8]

To have everything brilliantly lit was an important part of the Christmas decorating. As many lights and candles as could be found illuminated the house at night, red being the preferred color for holiday candles. "A great deal of lights are required, where fir and holly are much used, in table decoration, otherwise the effect is heavy and gloomy." [9] Candles were expensive but this was the time to be extravagant. The scene at Auburn plantation in Mathews County on the Chesapeake Bay included lighting in the hallways that was reminiscent of colonial illuminations:

> *"The rooms were decorated with holly and other evergreens and every [oil] lamp and candlestick was put in requisition. In addition to which, strips of boards were placed over the passages perforated with holes to hold additional lights. The doors inside were thrown open, and it was like an illumination."* [10]

Colorful banners and shields with seasonal symbols or sayings were suspended by ribbons. When it came to decorating, even the bedrooms received their share of attention.

As cities grew larger and forests grew farther away, city folk found themselves unable to stroll into the woods to gather Christmas greens. Quick to fill the void were the farmers bringing boughs of holly and other forest bounty to sell at the daily markets. The new fashion for Christmas trees added to the demand.

The Christmas Tree

Everyone, it seems, knows that the Christmas tree was a German tradi-

VICTORIAN TREE ORNAMENTS

Ornaments for Christmas trees during the nineteenth century were usually homemade and not intended to last from year to year. Most were distributed to the guests at the tree lighting party to be eaten on the spot or taken home as a gift. Many were accompanied by short poems or witty verses meant to be read aloud. Small toys, cookies, gilded nuts, scented sachets, tiny baskets of candy, and candle stubs or thin candles called tapers were tied or wired onto the stronger branches (ornament hooks did not come into the picture until 1892). Miniature flags were a popular decoration and so were cornucopias, conical shaped containers that held sweets. A very early description of Christmas tree ornaments (1832) included this eggshell basket:

"The cook had broken eggs carefully in the middle for some weeks past, that Charley might have the shells for cups; and these cups were gilded and coloured very prettily. We were all engaged in sticking on the last seven dozen of wax tapers, and in filling the gilded egg cups and gay paper cornucopiae with comfits, lozenges, and barley sugar. The tree was the top of a young fir, planted in a tub, which was ornamented with moss. Smart dolls and other whimsies glittered in the evergreen, and there was not a twig which had not something sparkling upon it." [11]

tion with roots in pagan festivals going back beyond the time of ancient Rome. Less well known is that this was a minor tradition confined mainly to the Alsace region between France and Germany, a tradition that did not spread to the rest of Germany until after 1750. Ironically, the German Christmas tree came to America from England.

No records from the Middle Ages mention a Christmas tree, but there is an old tradition of a "paradise tree" that sounds like a plausible ancestor. This paradise tree was a stage prop in the popular religious plays (called mystery plays) about Adam and Eve and it was hung, appropriately enough, with what passed for red apples. Although it would seem an oxymoron, December 24 was commonly celebrated as Adam and Eve's birthday—thus their association with Christmas. Those who see the paradise tree as the precursor to our Christmas tree claim, with some logic, that the apples evolved into our round ornaments. Another possible predecessor to the Christmas tree is the wooden pyramid form found in some parts of Germany, Switzerland, and Bohemia. People in these regions placed the wooden form on a table, tied bits of greenery on it, and decorated it with fruit, cookies, colored paper, and candles.

The earliest hint of the Christmas tree custom can be found in a sternly worded Alsatian (German) prohibition of 1561 forbidding anyone to "have for Christmas more than one bush of more than eight shoes' length." [12] Whether this was a fire precaution, a conservation measure, or something entirely different, we will probably never know. A few decades later, in 1605 (the year before the Jamestown adventurers sailed to Virginia), the first description of a decorated Christmas tree shows up. "At Christmas they set up fir-trees in the parlours at Strasbourg and hang thereon roses cut out of many-coloured paper, apples, wafers, gold-foil, sweets, &c."[13] The tradition spread slowly among wealthy, upper class Germans—they were certainly not common in average homes. Nor were they popular with everyone. One Scrooge-like German minister in Strasbourg deplored the practice.

"Among other trifles with which the people often occupy the Christmas time more than with God's word, is also the Christmas or fir tree, which they erect in the house, and hang with dolls and sugar and thereupon shake and cause to lose its bloom. Where the habit comes from, I know not. It is

a bit of child's play. . . Far better were it for the children to be dedicated to the spiritual cedar tree, Jesus Christ." [14]

Legend has it that the Christmas tree came to America with the German immigrants. This is true as far as it goes but it is important to remember that not all Germans celebrated Christmas and relatively few of those who did came from the part of Germany where Christmas trees were a sometime custom. There are many references to American Christmas trees—each competing to be the "first" in its state or region—and some are as early as the 1700s but this quaint German custom would probably have remained just that

Photo courtesy of The Winterthur Library: Joseph Downs Collection of Manuscripts and Printed Ephemera.

This is the earliest known depiction of a Christmas tree in America. A German immigrant, John Lewis Krimmel, sketched the picture in either 1812 or 1819 when he was visiting in Pennsylvania.

had it not been for the influence of an English queen. When Queen Victoria's German-born husband (and first cousin) Prince Albert of Saxe-Coburg-Gotha arranged for a fir tree to be brought from his homeland and decorated in 1841, it created a minor sensation throughout the English-speaking world.

Everyone knew of Queen Victoria's Christmas tree. A print of the royal family gathered about the Christmas tree at Windsor Castle appeared in the *Illustrated London News* in 1848 (see page 56), then in *Godey's Lady's Book* in

1850 and again ten years later. The six-foot fir tree sits on a table, each tier laden with a dozen or more lighted wax tapers. An angel with outstretched arms poses at the top. Gilt gingerbread ornaments and tiny baskets filled with sweets hang by ribbons from the branches. Clustered around the base of the tree are dolls and soldiers and toys. In 1855, Charles Dickens describes a tree that sounds remarkably like the Queen's or some other wealthy family's indulgence.

> *"I have been looking on, this evening, at a merry company of children assembled round that pretty German toy, a Christmas tree. The tree was planted in the middle of a great round table, and towered high above their little heads. It was brilliantly lighted by a multitude of little tapers; and everywhere sparkled and glittered with bright objects. There were rosy cheeked dolls, hiding behind the green leaves; there were real watches (with moveable hands, at least, and an endless capacity of being wound up) dangling from innumerable twigs; there were French-polished tables, chairs, bedsteads, wardrobes and eight-day clocks, and various other articles of domestic furniture (wonderfully made, in tin, at Wolverhampton), perched among the boughs, as if in preparation for some fairy housekeeping; there were jolly, broad-faced little men, much more agreeable in appearance than many real men—and no wonder, for their heads took off, and showed them to be full of sugarplums; there were fiddles and drums; there were tambourines, books, work-boxes, paintboxes, sweetmeat-boxes, peep-show boxes, all kinds of boxes; there were trinkets for the elder girls, far brighter than any grown-up gold and jewels; there were baskets and pin-cushions in all devices; there were guns, swords, and banners; there were witches standing in enchanted rings of paste-board, to tell fortunes; there were tee-totums, humming-tops, needle-holders; real fruit, made artificially dazzling with gold leaf; imitation apples, pears, and walnuts, crammed with surprises; in short, as a pretty child, before me, delightedly whispered to another pretty child, her bosom friend, 'There was everything, and more.'"* [15]

Victorian era Christmas trees were not just for admiring. They were an activity, usually the climax of a Christmas party involving children. When the tree candles were lit and the guests had gathered around, one person picked off the ornaments and passed them out. In some instances, each ornament had a name or a short verse attached to it indicating who was to receive it; in others, it

Photo courtesy of The Library of Virginia

A Christmas tree was the main event at a children's party. This print in <u>Harper's Weekly,</u> December 25, 1858, shows the father distributing the tree decorations to the young guests. Usually the ornaments were small toys, gingerbread cookies, or miniature baskets of candy, each with a personalized verse to be read aloud at the presentation. Note the decorations above the picture and the wreath on the inside *of the window—outdoor decorations did not exist until much later.*

was left to the discretion of the distributor. The little paper cornucopias filled with sweets and the cut-out cookies and the polished apples were quickly demolished, the toys or trinkets taken home, and the tree safely removed.

Prince Albert's Christmas tree certainly caught the public's imagination. It was not, however, the first German tree in England, as is commonly thought. Queen Victoria had seen one as a girl in 1832. Her Aunt Sophia had set up two "trees hung with lights and sugar ornaments. All the presents being placed around the tree," the little princess wrote excitedly in her diary. And long before that, Queen Charlotte, wife of George III, sent to her native Germany for a Christmas tree in 1789. With "bunches of sweetmeats, almonds, and raisins in papers, fruits, and toys most tastefully arranged" on its branches and illuminated by small wax candles, it seemed to Dr. John Watkins, the queen's physician, "a charming imported German custom."[16] Charming it may have been but it didn't stick. More than fifty years would pass before the custom took root in English and in American soil.

Once the royal seal of approval had been stamped solidly on the Christmas tree, the practice spread, slowly at first, throughout England and America and, to a lesser extent, to other parts of the world. Upper class Victorian Englishmen loved to imitate the royal family, and Americans followed suit. Larger floor-to-ceiling trees replaced the tabletop size. By 1909, the Forest Service was estimating that 5 million trees were cut, meaning as many as half of the families in America had one in their home.

To be sure, there had been Christmas trees in America before the Queen Victoria media blitz but virtually all these had involved Moravians or other German-born Americans and the custom had shown no sign of spreading beyond that narrow ethnic group. The writer of an 1825 article in *The Saturday Evening Post* mentions seeing trees in the windows of many houses in Philadelphia, a city with a large German population. Their "green boughs [were] laden with fruit, richer than the golden apples of the Hesperides, or the sparkling diamonds that clustered on the branches in the wonderful cave of Aladdin." Gilded apples hung from the branches as did marzipan ornaments, sugar cakes, miniature mince pies, spicy cookies cut from molds in the shape of stars, birds, fish, butterflies, and flowers. A woman visiting German friends in Boston in 1832 wrote about their unusual tree hung with gilded egg shell cups filled with candies. [17] In 1846 August Bodeker, a German American, set up Richmond's first tree in his apothecary shop window.

It was no different in Williamsburg. The first Christmas tree in that town—probably the first in Virginia—came courtesy of a young German-born professor at the College of William and Mary.

Charles Frederick Ernest Minnigerode was a native of the German state of Hesse. While still a student at the University of Giessen, he took part in an abortive uprising in 1834 against the repressive government and spent the next five years in prison for his pains. After his release he fled to America, making his way to Williamsburg to take a job teaching Latin and Greek. The young man struck up a strong friendship with Judge Nathaniel Beverly Tucker who lived a few blocks from the College. (The house has been restored by the Colonial Williamsburg Foundation.)

Minnigerode became a favorite with the whole family and the Tucker children soon nicknamed him "Minck." When the Judge invited him to spend

Christmas 1842 with them, he accepted gladly. No doubt feeling a little homesick for his native land, he asked Judge Tucker if he could prepare the children a Christmas tree after the German custom. Cutting off the top of an evergreen, he brought it into the parlor and showed the Tucker children how to make decorations: strings of popcorn, gilded nut shells, colored balls of paper, baskets of bonbons, and candle stubs wired to the ends of the branches.

Photo David M. Doody

Word of the beautiful Christmas tree spread fast. There were several parties for neighborhood children and young cousins came from as far away as Petersburg to see the marvel. Martha Page Vandegrift came from Gloucester County to visit when she was about twelve years old. She recalled the event many years later.

> *"He [Minnigerode] said his holiday wouldn't be complete without it and he wanted Chick [her friend, Cynthia Beverley Tucker] and me to see one for the first time. He set up an evergreen in the sitting room and decorated it with candles and bits of bright paper and <u>way</u> at the top of the branches he hung a gilded star. We children danced and shouted for joy when those candles were lit one by one. We'd never seen anything in the world so beautiful! I've never had a merrier Christmas than that one—never, ever—and I've had ninety-five of 'em!"* [18]

Private collection

Mrs. Vandegrift was right on the mark when she said that "the old judge enjoyed it as much as we did." He continued the Christmas tree custom the next year and every year for the rest of his life, marking the point at which the German custom became American.

One might have expected to see an earlier example of a Christmas tree in the western part of Vir-

Cynthia Beverley Tucker who, as a child in 1842, saw the German-born professor decorate Virginia's first Christmas tree.

ginia where German settlements date from at least 1727. After all, many of the Germans were Lutherans and Moravians who "kept Christmas" and some had been born in the old country where the old traditions were followed. But the Germans living in the Valley of Virginia during those years had not immigrated from the Alsace region where the Christmas tree custom originated. The first known Christmas tree in the western part of the state would not appear until 1855, in the home of a German immigrant in Staunton.

By mid-century Christmas trees were spreading into other homes with no known German connection. Robert E. Lee's children enjoyed a tabletop tree at their quarters at West Point, New York in 1853 when their father was Superintendent of the Military Academy. President Franklin Pierce set up a "German tree" in the White House in 1856. In Washington, D.C., Center Market was the place to buy greens and trees, and, since most of those trees came by the wagonload from Virginia or Maryland, the first White House tree may well have been cut in Virginia. During the worst winter of the Civil War, President and Mrs. Jefferson Davis decorated a Christmas tree and took it with presents to the Episcopalian home for orphans. Coincidentally, Minnigerode was on the scene for that Christmas tree as well. The Lutheran professor had

turned Episcopal minister and moved to Richmond's St. Paul's Church in 1856 where he became a friend and spiritual counselor to the Davises.

Newspapers and women's magazines like *Ladies' Home Journal, Godey's Lady's Book,* and *Ladies National Magazine* spread the Christmas tree custom to all ethnic groups and economic classes. The ever-popular *Godey's Lady's Book* ran a story just before the Civil War that described the "dressing" of the Christmas tree with detail enough for anyone to follow. This story is the first to tell of a tree reaching from floor to ceiling. Green baize fabric was to be tacked down to cover the floor, then a large ceramic jar was placed in the middle. The tree was held in place with wet sand and the whole base covered with green chintz to conceal the jar. A cushion of moss surrounded the base and presents were placed on the moss. Pieces of fine wire were passed through the bottom of tiny tapers (a small type of candle) and twisted under the branch to fasten them onto the tree. A drop of alcohol on each wick would make them light more quickly when the time came but first, the tree must be decorated with "long strings of bright red holly berries threaded like beads upon fine cord . . . festooned in graceful garlands from the boughs of the tree," bouquets of paper flowers, "tiny flags of gay ribbons," stars and shields of gilt paper, lace bags filled with colored candies, and knots of bright ribbon. On this particular tree, the parents contrived to place several dolls for the girls and, for the boy, a large cart with two horses "drove gayly among the top branches, as if each steed possessed the wings of Pegasus." Wooden animals romped on the moss. At the very top, an empty gilded bird cage waited for the canary that was to be one child's gift.[19]

Reality was less elaborate, especially during the war years. Those who followed the new fashion for Christmas trees had little with which to decorate during these hard times.

> *"It is a sad Christmas; cold and threatening snow. My two youngest children, however, have decked the parlor with evergreens, crosses, stars, etc. They have a cedar Christmas-tree but it is not burdened. Candy is held at $8 per pound . . . No merriment this Christmas."* [20]

It was not until after the Civil War that the Christmas tree custom flourished widely in the United States. During those years, the Christmas tree, along with Santa Claus, gift-giving, and the reading of Clement Moore's poem started to take over the Sunday School programs. For many children (and most adults), the first decorated tree they saw was not at home but at Sunday School.

During the last quarter of the nineteenth century, families that had Christmas trees loaded them with toys and edible ornaments and usually placed an angel or star at the top. Blown glass ornaments imported from Germany made their first appearance in the 1870s, followed quickly by American-made copies from a New York glassblower. Tiny American flags added splashes of patriotism. By the time Benjamin Harrison served as president, decorated Christmas trees had become widespread.

"I am an ardent believer in the duty we owe to ourselves as Christians to make merry to children at Christmas time," President Harrison explained, "and we shall have an old-fashioned Christmas tree for the grandchildren upstairs; and I shall be their Santa Claus myself. If my influence does for aught in this busy world let me hope that my example may be followed in every family in the land." [21]

By 1893, it probably was.

Santa Claus

The Dutch in New York enjoyed the Christmas season much the way the English did, by eating, drinking, and visiting, and with long parties. But the Dutch had something others did not: St. Nicholas.

The Dutch version of St. Nicholas travelled the land on the eve of December 6, his feast day, bringing candy or gifts to good children and switches for

the bad. Children who lived in the lower Rhineland (the area around the Dutch-German border) left hay outside for the great white horse he rode. An early woodcut from 1810 shows the tall saint in his bishop's garb with a purse in one hand and a birch rod in the other. He was originally pictured wearing red bishop's robes, appropriate enough as this saint was the fourth-century Bishop of Myra, a seaport in present day Turkey.

There is no hard proof to satisfy historians but legend tells us that Nicholas was persecuted during the reign of the Roman emperor Diocletian, imprisoned, and released when Constantine came to the throne. Nicholas supposedly died in 326 AD and was canonized in the ninth century after many miracles were attributed to him. The patron saint of children, "Sinterklaas," as the Dutch called him, became a minor figure in Dutch Christmas celebrations due to the proximity of his feast day.

This nineteenth-century wooden store figure of Santa Claus was carved by Charles Robb (1855-1904). Nearly four feet tall, it is part of the Abby Aldrich Rockefeller Folk Art Collection in Williamsburg.

In the United States, St. Nicholas was first given wider exposure by Washington Irving. In 1809, Irving's *Knickerbocker's History of New York* describes Santa Claus and how he flew over the treetops in a wagon full of toys. Clement C. Moore added the reindeer sleigh with his 1823 poem that begins, "'Twas the night before Christmas and all through the house." He secularized Santa, blending him in with folk figures like elves and fairies. To Moore, Santa looked like a stout, jolly elf dressed in fur rather than the tall bishop in red robes.

Popular American artist Thomas Nast—a German, of course! born in Landau, Germany and brought to the United States at six—refined Santa's image in *Harper's Weekly* where a different drawing of the jolly old elf was published almost every year from the Civil War until 1886. Nast was the first to relate Santa to patriotism with his portrayal of Santa giving gifts to Union soldiers and it was he who added the workshop where Santa made his toys.

Southerners were not about to let Santa succumb to Nast's Northern propaganda. Mary A. M'Crimmon gave voice to many Southern mothers when she wrote this poem explaining why Santa could not bring treats while the war raged. The Yankees, some said, were holding him prisoner.

> *"This happened one Christmas, I'm sorry to write,*
> *Our ports were blockaded, and Santa, tonight,*
> *Will hardly get down here; for if he should start,*
> *The Yankees would get him, unless he was smart;*
> *They beat all the men in creation to run,*
> *And if they could get him, they'd think it fine fun*
> *To put him in prison, and steal the nice toys*
> *He started to bring to our girls and our boys.*
> *But try not to mind it—tell over your jokes—*
> *Be gay and be cheerful, like other good folks;*
> *For if you remember to be good and kind,*
> *Old Santa next Christmas will bear it in mind."* [22]

Even before the Civil War, "stockings were hung by the chimney with care, in hopes that Saint Nicholas soon would be there" with an orange and some candy on Christmas morning. These stockings were nothing more than the child's usual socks hung over the fireplace mantel. Santa usually dropped

The American Santa Claus had several creators but political cartoonist Thomas Nast, a German-born Ameri-can, gave us his appearance in a series of illustrations in <u>Harper's Weekly</u> *that spanned three decades. Above, one of his earliest pictures (1866); below, perhaps his best known (1881).*

an orange into the toe. "We would hang up our stockings and they were always filled, but not with expensive things, as in these days. A bunch of raisins, an orange, a stick or two of peppermint candy and an alabaster doll, or book, made us happy." [23]

In the 1850s, "Santa impersonators" began to make annual appearances in the larger stores, funded by merchants who were quick to grasp the gift-giving connection. By 1887, Richmond children counted the start of the Christmas season from the moment when the confectionery shop at Third and Broad Streets set a large plaster of Paris statue of "St. Nick" in its front window.

Gifts

While the custom of exchanging wrapped Christmas presents has its origins in the nineteenth century, this 1577 stanza by Thomas Tusser, the English writer and poet, suggests it could have been a revival of a much older practice.

> *"At Christmas of Christ many Carols we sing,*
> *and give many gifts in the joy of that King."* [24]

Gift-giving was a minor part of the Virginia Christmas tradition in the colonial period, limited largely to tips to servants or insignificant gifts to little children. During the nineteenth century, the custom took on a life of its own.

One of the earlier instances of adults exchanging gifts involved Virginians Meriwether Lewis and William Clark and took place in the wilderness of present day Oregon. The expedition spent a miserable winter at Fort Clatsop, which the men built at the mouth of the Columbia River. It was a wet, disagreeable day but somehow, they managed a little Christmas entertainment in the Virginia fashion, shooting Christmas guns, singing, and exchanging makeshift gifts. One of the men made Clark a pair of moccasins, and Captain Clark wrote , "I received a present of . . . two Dozen white weazils tails of the Indian woman [Sacajawea] and some black root of the Indians before their departure." The captains gave the men a ration of tobacco; those who did not smoke received a handkerchief. [25]

By the second quarter of the century, gift giving between members of the family had arrived in force. From the start, most gifts were purchased, not made at home, and some stores in the cities stayed open until midnight to accommodate shoppers. Unwrapped gifts were placed under or tied onto the tabletop Christmas tree; wrapped gifts might be set on the sideboard in the family dining room, to be opened after prayers and breakfast. Virginia accounts from the 1870s and 1880s mention tea sets, dolls and doll furniture,

This print from 1882 shows a storekeeper getting ready for Christmas shoppers.

cradles, painted wooden carts, toy swords, Swiss playing cards, ice skates, sleds, Barlow knives, and an iron horse and carriage.

Presents during the Civil War were handmade affairs, even for the relatively well-to-do, such as President Jefferson Davis's family. Mrs. Davis recalled their last Christmas at the Confederate White House in 1864, and the presents they made for their slaves and family members.

> "At last quiet settled on the household and the older members began to stuff stockings with molasses candy, red apples, an orange, small whips plaited by the family with high-colored crackers, worsted reins knitted at home, paper dolls, teetotums made of large horn buttons and a match which would spin indefinitely, balls of worsted rags wound hard and covered with old kid gloves, a pair of pretty woolen gloves for each, either cut out of cloth and embroidered on the back or knitted by some deft hand out of homespun wool... On Christmas morning the children awoke early and came in to see their toys. They were followed by the Negro women, who one after another 'caught' us by wishing us merry Christmas before we could say it to them,

which gave them a right to a gift. Of course, there was a present for everyone, small though it might be, and one who had been born and brought up at our plantation was vocal in her admiration of a gay handkerchief. As she left the room she ejaculated: 'Lord knows Mistress knows our insides—she just got the very thing I wanted.' [26]

Mrs. Davis received some baby clothes, a pincushion, and six cakes of soap; the President had some gloves and a handkerchief.

Gingerbread

Gingerbread—spicy, fragrant, and warm from the brick oven—it is hard to find an early cookbook without at least one recipe for this popular treat. The word goes back to the Middle Ages—perhaps further—but ever since the fifteenth century, the ingredients for this simple cake have included molasses and ginger.

Traditionally, gingerbread cakes were made small and cut into the shapes of animals, men, or letters of the alphabet. The European nobility was fond of gilding them with real gold leaf. Only after the colonial period did they come to be called "cookies," and only in the United States.

Gingerbread has long been identified with Christmas. Gingerbread cookie ornaments hung from the branches of the earliest American Christmas trees; children received gingerbread animals and whole gingerbread families as Christmas gifts; a popular children's book called *Giles Gingerbread* was listed in a 1768 *Virginia Gazette* advertisement as a good gift for children. Even in the darkest days of the Civil War, Southern mothers managed to scrape up enough ingredients to bake fanciful gingerbread toys for the little ones to play with and eat.

"At night I treated our little party to tea and ginger cakes—two very rare indulgences; and but for the sorghum, grown in our own fields, the cakes would be an impossible indulgence. Nothing but the well-ascertained fact that Christmas comes but once a year would make such extravagance at all excusable." [27]

More recently, decorating gingerbread houses has become a popular Christmas activity for the whole family.

Christmas Cards

Some say the Christmas card was inspired by "Christmas pieces," decoratively written samplers worked by English schoolboys in the eighteenth and nineteenth centuries to show parents how much they had improved their penmanship, but there is little indication that the transfer was that direct. The first card was printed in England by John C. Horsley at the request of Henry Cole, the well-known museum pioneer who founded the Victoria and Albert Museum, when he could not find the time to write a Christmas greeting to all his friends and relatives. It was the first and the last time he did so, perhaps because of the outspoken criticism of his card. Prohibitionists condemned the scene showing a family (including a child) drinking Christmas cheer. Nonetheless the card idea caught on and spread to America.

Christmas cards did not become popular in the northern United States until around 1862. In 1875, immigrant Louis Prang—German of course—snatched the market away from the British with his cheaper, domestic cards. In Virginia, as in the rest of the South, the wartime poverty and destruction left little room for such extravagances.

Photo courtesy of The Valentine Museum of the Life and History of Richmond

The earliest known Christmas season greeting card received in Virginia, this card was printed in England, probably in the 1850s.

Christmas Guns and Fireworks

The practice of firing guns into the air on Christmas and New Year's, long known as Christmas Guns or "shooting in the New Year," refused to fade, much to the consternation of those who lived in urban areas. On Dec. 25, 1804, Robert Mitchell, Mayor of Richmond, reported to the governor in frustration,

> "I wrote Maj'r Wolfe to furnish a Serg't Guard out of the militia, in order to aid our city Patrol to patrol the city . . . during the Christmas Holydays, which has been complyed with, but it does appear to me to be impossible to prevent firing what is called Christmas Guns, being an old established custom, although there is an ordinance of the city police fixing a fine of 5 s. for every offence of firing Guns within this city." [28]

Indeed, the custom was spreading. On the Lewis and Clark expedition, the men celebrated Christmas 1804 in Mandan Indian village by firing their guns into the air; the next year, at Fort Clatsop near the mouth of the Columbia River, they exchanged makeshift gifts and fired their guns again. "We were awaked at daylight by a discharge of firearms which was followed by a song from the men, as a compliment to us on the return of Christmas, which we have always been accustomed to observe as a day of rejoicing," wrote Captain William Clark. A few days later, "We were awakened at an early hour by the discharge of a volley of small-arms to salute the new year. This is the only mode of doing honor to the day which our situation permits."[29] Both Clark and Meriwether Lewis were born and raised near Charlottesville, Virginia and both had, no doubt, grown up with the sound of Christmas guns ringing in their ears.

Some towns tried to regulate Christmas fireworks, with mixed results. In 1887, Staunton set aside eleven days when fireworks would be permitted.

To some children, "Christmas guns" had a different meaning. Ellen Mordecai recalled her childhood on a plantation in the 1830s:

> *"I must not forget the Christmas guns. These were bladders, which the men always saved for us, and the women washed and prepared them. We would blow them up with a quill and hang them up in a dry place, and Christmas morning we would take them down and hold them to the fire until they were swelled out taut; then we would run with them to the bedroom doors and jump on them and cry out, 'Christmas Gift!'"* [30]

During the Civil War, when Richmond bulged with refugees, soldiers, and transients, the Christmas Guns provided a bit of cheer when little else was available.

> *"We have quite a merry Christmas in the family; and a compact that no unpleasant word shall be uttered . . . The family were baking cakes and pies until late last night, and to-day we shall have full rations. I have found enough celery in the little garden for dinner. Last night and this morning the boys have been firing Christmas guns incessantly—no doubt pilfering from their fathers' cartridge-boxes. There is much jollity and some drunkenness in the streets, notwithstanding the enemy's pickets are within an hour's march to the city."* [31]

Although there are isolated references to Christmas guns outside Virginia—in Baltimore, the Carolinas, and New York—in the 1800s, the practice did not catch on in the North. On Christmas Day, 1871, the *New York Times* sniffed, "The distracting reports of fire-arms and fire-works, an absurd southern custom, has at times been hideous." [32]

From gunpowder to fireworks was an easy step and by the nineteenth century, the repertoire of Christmas noise included both. In Richmond, a diarist noted that "The boys are firing Chinese crackers everywhere, and no little gunpowder is consumed in commemoration of the day." [33]

An amateur poet remembers his Christmas fireworks before the war,
> *"We went to the pond for skating*
> *To the stable to take a ride,*
> *And we found new joys awaiting,*
> *To whatever spot we hied,*
> *But the climax of my story*
> *Was that evening's fireworks show!*
> *Went out in a blaze of glory—*
> *That Christmas long ago!"* [34]

The Valley of Virginia

As the frontier and its hazards moved further west, life became both easier and more complex for farmers in the Valley of Virginia. Added to the mountain melting pot were English Episcopalians and revivalist groups like Baptists. The former celebrated the Christmas season, the latter, who followed the Puritans in morality and in their simplified form of Christianity, did not. The Germans remained highly fragmented throughout the nineteenth century: Lutherans and Reformed took their worship style and approach to life from the Rhineland and the Moravians emphasized the Baby Jesus, while Mennonites, Amish, and Brethren (who continued to immigrate into the Valley of Virginia) treated the day like any other. The Scotch-Irish from Ulster held fast to their stern Presbyterianism.

But the Lutheran Germans, along with the Episcopalians and the handful of Catholics that were there, celebrated Christmas in both religious and secular ways. The religious Christmas involved a service at the parish church with holy communion, the singing of Advent hymns and Christmas carols, and the decoration of the church interior. At home, they followed either the early Virginia customs of "merry Old England" or the German customs of the Rhineland.

Refugee Alice West Allen, whose family fled the fighting in the Valley of Virginia, recalled Christmas in 1864. "We were delighted when we got to Richmond. The next morning our aunt took us out shopping; and as each of us had one hundred dollars to spend, we thought we could give presents to all at home. We soon found that toys and candy were as costly as food." [35]

At least as early as the 1850s, many German residents of the Valley of Virginia celebrated the Christmas season with the unique custom of "belsnickeling." [36] The tradition's origins are murky but the name comes from the Germans of the Palatinate region where Belznickel, or Saint Nicholas, brought small gifts for good children. In the Valley of Virginia, this evolved into bands of costumed adults wandering on foot or horseback from house to house during the day or night, making as much noise as humanly possible. Belsnickelers disguised themselves with old feed sacks, salt bags, paper bags, stockings, or pillowcases for masks. The trick was for the residents to guess who was behind the costume. Customs varied from community to community, and the practice was not appreciated among the Brethren, the Mennonites, and others who did not observe Christmas. Sometimes the Belsnicklers unmasked after the guessing, sometimes they were served spirits or food. In some areas the practice was restricted to Christmas Eve; in others, it went on for the twelve days of Christmas.

In certain regions, particularly in Scotch-Irish settlements south of Winchester in Augusta and Rockbridge counties, a similar ritual developed called "shanghai-ing." During daylight hours, a parade of shanghai-ers wearing disguises and making noise would parade through the streets of towns. In 1870, shanghais marched through Staunton on Christmas Day; in 1889 and 1890 there were Shaghai parades in Greenville with as many as 52 costumed marchers.

Photo courtesy of Museum of American Frontier Culture

By the 1850s, Christmas customs similar to today's had arrived in the Valley of Virginia. Children were hanging stockings for Santa Claus to fill and waiting for the belsnickler invasion. A local newspaper published articles each year about Christmas customs around the world and told the legends of Saint Nicholas. All newspapers ran advertisements of Christmas gifts: especially books, but also jewelry, cosmetics, sewing boxes, paperweights, purses, and oil lamps. Still, gift giving was not the focal point of the season and many children were delighted with nothing more than a few coins and some candy.

Both belsnickeling and shanghai-ing declined in the twentieth century and finally disappeared after World War II.

A Slave Celebration

In the ante-bellum South, no one looked forward to Christmas more than the slaves. The meager Christmas privileges accorded to slaves in the eighteenth century had grown into inalienable rights by the nineteenth and more than one scholar specializing in African-American history has remarked on the universality of Christmas celebration. Not even the harshest master dared deny his "people" their due: a minimum of a three-day holiday and extra pro-

Photo by Cathy Dixson

The Executive Mansion, built in 1813, is the oldest continuously occupied governor's residence in the United States. It is listed on both the Virginia Landmarks Register and the National Register of Historic Places, and it was proclaimed a National Historic Landmark in 1988. Twice fire nearly destroyed the mansion. At the end of the Civil War, Union troops saved the building from burning by climbing onto the shingled roof and beating out the flames, a good deed somewhat tarnished by their subsequent looting of the house. Half a century later, a governor's son, a sparkler, and a dry Christmas tree caused major damage to the 1906 wing.

"He [Minnigerode] set up an evergreen in the sitting room and decorated it with candles and bits of bright paper and <u>way</u> at the top of the branches he hung a gilded star..." Strings of popcorn and baskets of bonbons were essential decorations for the Victorian Christmas tree. See pages 68-69 for the story of Williamsburg's 1842 tree.

Photos by David M. Doody

Photo courtesy of Museum of the Confederacy, photo by Katherine Wetzel

Curators at the Museum of the Confederacy used two eyewitness accounts describing Christmas trees in 1864 to re-create the above tree.

In her memoirs written in 1896 Varina Davis tells of the "orphan's tree" she and President Jefferson Davis assembled for the children at the Episcopalian Home. She relates how, on "Christmas Eve a number of young people were invited to come and string apples and popcorn for the tree; a neighbor very deft in domestic arts had tiny candle molds made and furnished all the candles for the tree. However, the puzzle and triumph of all was the construction of a large number of cornucopias. ... The beauty of these homemade things astonished us all, for they looked quite 'custom made'..."

Isobel Maury, a Clay Street neighbor of the Davises, also had a tree that year. Hers had on top "two flags, our Confederate and our Battle Flag...[picture of] General Lee, bless his soul, was hung immediately below."

Bassett Hall, the Williamsburg home of Mr. and Mrs. John D. Rockefeller, Jr., was furnished in the 1930s and 1940s with an eclectic mixture of antiques, folk art, and contemporary pieces to create a comfortable home. The Christmas decorations and table settings are appropriate to those decades.

Photos courtesy of Colonial Williamsburg Foundation

Photos courtesy of Colonial Williamsburg Foundation

The kissing ball, a variation on the much older English mistletoe custom, evolved during the nineteenth century. A boxwood kissing ball hangs in the hall of Carter's Grove, a James River plantation restored and enlarged in the 1920s and 1930s by Mr. and Mrs. Archibald McCrea. Although built in the eighteenth century, the house is furnished according to its 1930s appearance and reflects a Christmas of that time.

Herb kissing ball.

Pomegranate, lemons, and cranberries.

The tasty pomegranate was far more appreciated by our colonial forebears than it is today. With its hard rind and crimson pulp, it is a perfect Christmas decoration on the plate or wreath, but it remains a curiosity in many parts of the country. The word pomegranate derives from the Latin 'pomum granatum,' meaning apple with many grains or seeds. It was familiar to the ancient Hebrews (see the Song of Solomon) and to the ancient Greeks (see the myth of Persephone). Islamic invaders introduced the pomegranate to their expanding empire, notably Spain, where the powerful kingdom of Granada took its name from the fruit. Visitors to Williamsburg are often surprised to see pomegranates in the Christmas decorations, but the fruit did grow in Tidewater Virginia during the colonial period. Mark Catesby, the famous naturalist and artist, noted that pomegranates grew "in great perfection in the Gardens of the Hon. William Byrd, Esq.; in the freshes of the James river."

American holly, ilex opaca.

Osage, orange, rosemary.

Photos courtesy of Colonial Williamsburg Foundation

Pomegranate seeds exposed.

Pineapple, lady apples, and pine cones.

As the holiday season lengthened, Colonial Williamsburg's outdoor decorating began making greater use of dried materials and other long lasting objects, such as (from left to right, top to bottom) garlic, wood shavings, tin mugs, reproduction playing cards, seashells, and blown eggs. Many of these photographs illustrate another recent trend: the use of items that relate to the building's original purpose. The playing cards decorate a former tavern for example, and the wreath of blown eggs is fastened to the window of a kitchen outbuilding.

1951

1974

1983

1984

1993

1998

Visitors return to Williamsburg's Historic Area year after year to see the outdoor decorations. Pictured here is the house of George Wythe, signer of the Declaration of Independence and law professor of Thomas Jefferson, as it appeared over five decades.

visions. Ex-slave Silas Jackson remembers his owner—"a meaner man was never born in Virginia—brutal, wicked, hard"— yet even this master gave each slave "ten dollars at Christmas time extra, besides his presents." [37]

Three days was the shortest holiday. Many received five days or the week between Christmas and New Year's Day; some longer than that. Interestingly, some masters in Virginia and other parts of the South resurrected the old English yule log tradition—it had never been part of America's early Christmas celebration—and declared a holiday from work for as long as the log burned. By cutting the thickest tree trunk in the woods and soaking it in water before delivering it to the master's house, slaves could ensure that their holiday ran a good deal longer than a week.

Good food and Christmas were synonymous for black Virginians as well as white. "We was given flour an' sugar an' coffee an' butter an' whiskey an' things." remembers Harriet, who had been a slave in her youth in Tidewater, Virginia. Others remember roast pig, turkey, game, plum-pudding, baked yams, and whiskey. Levi Pollard of Charlotte County told the WPA interviewer who questioned him about his childhood as a slave, "Sometimes dey would be a little extra, but us always got a peck er flour, a whole ham, 5 lbs. real cane sugar, en every body winter clothes." [38]

YULE LOG

*F*rom the old Norse word for wheel, *Juul*, comes the English word Yule, now a synonym for the Christmas season. The custom of burning a great log in the fireplace during the winter solstice has Scandinavian and Druidic origins but it never caught on in the United States except on ante-bellum plantations and in places like Williamsburg where reviving forgotten traditions was central to the holiday celebration.

Traditions vary but often the large log is coated with herbs or doused with wine in what must be seen as lingering remnants of pagan libations. Many superstitions concerning luck for the New Year go with the burning of the Yule log: it must burn for twelve days for good fortune, or it must be lit with the charred remains of its predecessor, for example. The custom declined in European cities where coal replaced wood, and trees, let alone thick logs, became unavailable.

Christmas was the only time of the year that slaves were permitted—even encouraged—to drink spirits. Drunkenness was overlooked. The eighteenth-century tutor, Philip Fithian, noted on Christmas Day that "the Fellow who makes the Fire in our School Room, drest very neatly in green, but almost drunk, entered my chamber with three or four profound Bows."[39] He gave him a tip and dismissed him quickly. Most plantation owners sent along a keg of whisky or barrel of hard cider to the slave quarters with the holiday food.

Presents from the master were expected. The old English Christmas box tradition, a tip of a few coins, had metamorphosed into Christmas gifts for everyone, usually clothes and shoes but often money, handkerchiefs, tobacco, and candy and toys for the youngsters. A game grew up in the plantation house whereby a house slave tried to "catch" a member of the white family on

The illustration, sketched in the summer of 1853 in Lynchburg, Virginia, by Lewis Miller, shows how slaves celebrated on special occasions.

Christmas morning, calling out "Christmas gift!" before the other could see him. If he succeeded, he was entitled to a tip or gift.

The custom spread through the black community beyond the house servants and sometimes white children would join in to "catch" an adult with the demand, "Christmas Gift!" After the Civil War the game persisted in some areas of the South, although it began to resemble Halloween trick-or-treating more than anything else. When he moved from Virginia to Alabama in 1881, a disapproving Booker T. Washington was astonished at the turn this game had taken.

> *"The first thing that reminded us that Christmas had arrived was the 'foreday' visits of scores of children rapping at our doors, asking for 'Chris'mus gifts! Chris'mus gifts!' Between the hours of two o'clock and five o'clock in the morning I presume that we must have had a half-hundred such calls. This custom prevails throughout this portion of the South today."* [40]

Others remembered the game more fondly. On Christmas Day in 1857, Amanda Virginia Edmonds noted in her diary, "Christmas Gift was heard from every tongue this morning before we hardly saw the first gleam of morning in the far east."[41]

There was another reason for slaves to celebrate at Christmas, a reason that had nothing to do with religion. By long custom, slaves that had been "hired-out" to another plantation or factory came home on Christmas Eve. Hiring contracts typically ran from New Year's Day to Christmas, giving Christmas the added poignancy of a family reunion. Ninety-eight-year-old Fannie Berry, who had been a slave in Virginia in her youth, remembered:

> *"Slaves lived jus' fo' Christmas to come round. Start gittin' ready de fus' snow fall. Commence to savin' nuts and apples, fixin' up party clothes, snitchin' lace an' beads fum de big house. General celebratin' time, you see, 'cause husbands is comin' home to see dey new babies. Ev'ybody happy."* [42]

Of course, the flip side to this was the knowledge that men hired out for the coming year would be leaving on New Year's Day, not to be seen again for a year. Depending upon one's prospects, New Year's Day (or "hirin' out day") could be a time of anxiety and sorrow.

The Christmas season often brought a taste of freedom too, as many masters permitted their slaves to travel to neighboring towns or plantations to visit family and friends and attend other festivities. Often masters would let "their people" use the barn for a big dance, called a "frolic;" otherwise the largest house in the quarters would have to do. Sometimes the master and his family would put in an appearance.

> *"Seems like he got as much fun out of it as us did," remembered Louise Jones, a former slave from Emporia, Virginia. "Let de men go in de saw mill an' put together a great platform an' bring it to de barn fo' us to dance on. Den come de music, de fiddles an' de banjos, de Jews harp, an' all dem other things," like homemade drums, bones, flutes, and whistles. "Sech dancin' you never did see befo'. . . . An' we sho' used to have a good time. Yes, sir. . . . Settin' all 'round was dem big demi-jonahs of whiskey what Marsa done give us. An' de smell of roast pigs an' chicken comin' fum de quarters made ev'ybody feel good. Wasn't nothin' we ain' had Christmas-time."* [43]

During the day, black children and adults would gather for religious services, singing, and story-telling or "play ring games, jump rope an' dance." Some would seize the opportunity to work for themselves, weaving baskets, knitting socks, or making quilts to sell. Although slave marriages were not legally recognized in the South, slaves did marry, often at Christmas time.

Photo courtesy of Colonial Williamsburg Foundation

"Boys and girls in their Sunday best, would parade down the line of cheering well-wishers, join hands, and 'jump the broomstick.' " [44]

A Northern infantryman learned how Virginia slaves celebrated Christmas when he attended their festivities near Camp Lyons, Virginia.

"You have probably read accounts…representing the numerous pleasures indulged in by negroes during holidays, when they are allowed the time to spend to their own satisfaction, in dancing, visiting, etc. Well, hearing that such an occasion was to take place on a small scale about 2 miles from camp, and wishing to see how it was passed off, I concluded to attend. I went. The scene of dance and festivities was a large hut, and we arrived there about 10 o'clock, starting away from camp right after roll-call. The room was pretty comfortably filled with the 'culled gemman' and their 'ladie lubs' to the accompanying music of the banjo. A man calling 'all hands around,' 'change partners,' 'form circle through the center,' etc. were the order of the evening and gaily did the merry voices resound through the room. As we arrived at the happy assemblage, the joyful ceremony of the rites of marriage was being performed. The happy couple stood there with their bright rows of ebony glancing in every which way. After remaining a while wended our way campwards…" [45]

General John B. Gordon's memoirs include a short history of Christmas in Virginia.

"The Southern people from their earliest history had observed Christmas as the great holiday season of the year. It was the time of times, the longed-for period of universal and innocent but boundless jollification among young and old. In towns and on plantations, purse-strings were loosened and restraints relaxed—so relaxed that even the fun-loving negro slaves were permitted to take upon them, and before daylight to storm 'de white folks' houses with their merry calls 'Christmas gift, master!' 'Christmas gift, everybody!' [46]

A member of the planter aristocracy waxed nostalgically for the good old days when his family's slaves celebrated the holiday.

"There was almost sure to be a negro wedding during the holidays. The ceremony might be performed in the dining room or in the hall by the master, or in one of the quarters by a colored preacher; but it was a festive occasion, and the dusky bride's trousseau had been arranged by her young mistress, and the [white] family was on hand to get fun out of the entertainment, and to recognize by their presence the solemnity of the tie." [47]

Booker T. Washington, a Virginian who became the most influential African-American leader of his era, described Christmas in the slave quarters in his autobiography.

> *"During the days of slavery it was a custom quite generally observed throughout all the Southern states to give the coloured people a week of holiday at Christmas, or to allow the holiday to continue as long as the "yule log" lasted. The male members of the race, and often the female members, were expected to get drunk... At night, during Christmas week, they usually had what they called a "frolic," in some cabin on the plantation. This meant a kind of rough dance, where there was likely to be a good deal of whiskey used..."* [48]

In words that echo the Puritan ministers of two centuries past, Booker T. Washington railed against the drinking and the "widespread hilarity" that accompanied this Christian holiday. What he lamented most was that "The sacredness of the season seemed to have been almost wholly lost sight of." At his school, the Tuskegee Institute, he tried to put things right. "[W]e made a special effort to teach our students the meaning of Christmas, and to give them lessons in its proper observance." In what must have been the precursor to Habitat for Humanity, Washington noted

> *"the unselfish and beautiful way in which our graduates and students spend their time in administering to the comfort and happiness of others, especially the unfortunate. Not long ago some of our young men spent a holiday in rebuilding a cabin for a helpless coloured woman who is about seventy-five years old."* [49]

After the Civil War turned slaves into freedmen who could legally own firearms, they joined the noisy custom of Christmas guns. As the century progressed, firecrackers became the preferred noisemaker with boys black and white. Booker T. Washington wrote of his sadness in visiting a rural black family where the only Christmas gifts the children had were firecrackers. Another observer noted that some poor black children made their own firecrackers by "blowing up hog bladders, tying them tight, and popping them in the flames of a fire." [50]

In urban areas, where city folk could not easily collect their own greenery or cut their own trees, they shopped for Christmas greens at their local market—in Richmond, the Sixth Street Market. Most of the evergreens purchased during the last quarter of the nineteenth century were gathered by black farmers living on the outskirts of the cities where there were large tracts of forest nearby. Holly bushes, pine and cedar boughs, clusters of mistletoe, and other native greenery became an important seasonal replacement for the usual fresh fruits and vegetables they usually sold. Some enterprising families sold home-made tree stands in their market booths as well.

A Richmond woman buys holly from a peddler at a farmer's market in this illustration from the cover of <u>Harper's Weekly</u> on Christmas Day, 1875.

Holiday Meals

By the middle of the nineteenth century, the sumptuousness of earlier dinners had become unfashionable. Gone were the symmetrically arranged profusion of more dishes than anyone could possibly taste. Many Virginians were adopting the simpler dining styles from Europe: the French fashion where the table cloth remained on the table throughout the entire meal, or the Russian style, called "service à la russe," that banished nearly everything from the dinner table except the individual place settings, a centerpiece, and the dessert. Rejecting the "immense multiplicity of dishes which every dinner-giver was obliged to produce," Virginians turned to the easier method of having their servants or slaves carve from the sideboard and serve one dish at a time to each guest.[51] Fashion now dictated centerpieces of fresh flowers and candelabra over the old elaborate glass pyramids and pastoral scenes dotted with sugar figures.

Photo courtesy of Colonial Williamsburg Foundation

Some dining customs did not change. The fruit and sweetmeat pyramids of colonial days never fell out of favor in Virginia. "[There were] many little iced cakes and rosy apples in pyramids," recalled Mrs. Harrison, the wife of President Jefferson Davis' secretary, in her Civil War memoirs.[52] And many Virginia families like the Harrisons and the Bollings, quoted below, clung fast to the old-fashioned English manners.

"There was no dream of war or trouble of any kind . . ." writes Julia Calvert Bolling Cabell in her recollections of the last Christmas at Bolling Hall before the War. "After the dishes were taken off, the top table cloth was removed—then Uncle Dan'll with snow white hair and a bright red waist-coat which he only wore at Xmas brought in the splendid "Silver Cross" which he placed in the centre of the table and the tall pyramid of rich fruit cake about two and a half feet high beautifully iced and a delicate wreath of holly twined around from bottom to top, with a bunch of holly and mistletoe at the top. Then there were mince-pies, lemon puddings, blanc-mange, cus-

tards and jellies all topped with Sylabub. . . Later on we were all again summoned to the Dining room. On the table was the beautiful old punch-bowl of rarest porcelain, baskets of eggs, pitchers of rich milk sugar and nutmeg in a silver grator and <u>several</u> black bottles with T. Bolling on the glass and containing Brandy or "Old Jamaica rum" how old I know not. . . After drinking healths and seeing the fires burning low, we said Good Night and went back to the "Island" at a brisk pace over the sparkling snow in the bright moon-light and this was the last gathering to celebrate Xmas at Bolling Hall, Va." [53]

The main dinner was usually served after church in the middle of the day. Before the war, plantation fare resembled that of colonial days: Oysters, wild turkeys, ducks, venison, beef, and hams are mentioned repeatedly, as are oranges, figs, and grapes. Pineapples, though not as rare as they had been during the colonial period, were still a special treat on any Christmas table.

Punch, the holiday beverage of colonial times, gave way to egg nog, a beverage made with raw egg yolks, whipped egg whites, milk, sugar, brandy, and rum. Each family had its special recipe that was handed down through the generations and carefully replicated year after year. Egg nog was usually served before breakfast and all day long and, unlike most alcohol, was considered a suitable drink for the ladies. More than one Virginia belle could have written this entry in her diary for December 25th: "Ches, Bettie and I have a joyful eggnog drink—I really got tight." [54]

*S*outhern *soldiers sorely missed their traditional egg nog and other spirits on Christmas Day. This simple lament by a soldier of the 12th Virginia in his letter to his family expressed what everyone was thinking.*

"Christmas day [was] the poorest ever spent, no egg nog, no turkey, no mince pie, nothing to eat or drink but our rations. We all talk of home today and wish to be there." [55]

Christmas during the War Between the States

Father Christmas "made a mourning wreath instead of his holly and mistletoe," lamented *Godey's Lady's Book* in December of 1862. The widespread death and destruction caused by the Civil War fell heaviest on Virginia, where more battles were fought than in any other state. Richmond, the capital of the Confederate States of America, swelled to four times its pre-war size as government workers, refugees, businessmen, and soldiers crowded its streets and filled its hotels, hospitals, and homes.

The first Christmas of the war found Virginians optimistic about the Confederacy's ultimate victory and hopeful that the fighting would soon end; succeeding years brought hunger, death, and mourning. There were thousands like Mary Boykin Chesnut, who, having just learned of the death of a close friend, could not face the usual celebrations. "The servants rush in — "Merry Christmas," &c &c &c — I covered my face and wept." [56]

In general, there was little fighting done at Christmas time, not because of religious constraints but because of the weather. Soldiers on both sides would build shelters for winter quarters and huddle by fires until the spring thaw. Throughout the war, civilians struggled to provide a festive dinner for the troops, in the field and in the hospital.

Photo courtesy of Massachusetts Commandery Military Order of the Loyal Legion and the US Army Military History Institute

This may well be the room described by Cornelia Hancock in her diary in 1864: "Christmas is over. We had it to perfection here, a splendid dinner for 1400 men . . .the dinner was set in the Government kitchen where 400 can be seated at once. The hall was decorated tastefully with evergreens and was really pretty as a picture. It was photographed, I believe." Hancock, a Quaker nurse, was working that year at City Point, Grant's main supply depot and the hub of Union activity in Virginia. [57]

"We read in the Richmond papers of the thousands and thousands of boxes that had been passed en route to the army, sent by the ladies of Richmond and other cities, but few found their way to us," wrote one soldier in Fredericksburg. "The greater part of them were for the troops from the far South who were too distant from their homes to receive anything from their own families." [58]

"It seemed to me I lived a week during the twenty four hours which constituted Christmas," wrote Phebe Yates Pember, a Jewish widow who came to Virginia from South Carolina to take charge of Chimborazo Hospital. Although Christmas held no religious significance for Mrs. Pember, Southern Jews tended to observe the secular part of their neighbors' holidays so she was quite familiar with Christmas expectations. And Mrs. Pember was not about to allow her patients to miss their share of Christmas cheer. "We made twenty four gallons of Egg-Nogg inviting all in the whole Division to come and drink and gave to each a good sized cake. At two o'clock having roasted a dozen turkeys and seven gallons of oysters we shared them out and hoped that each man got his share." Later in the evening, Mrs. Pember attended a Christmas dinner party where, "with true Virginia hospitality, they had not only invited me, but requested me to fill the two vacant chairs by my side." They dined at seven, then went to the home of one of the doctors "to see the Christmas tree on which I found my Christmas gift pretty enough to be most acceptable and simple enough to preclude all feelings of obligation." [59]

Homesickness and worry about their loved ones plagued Southern soldiers. Philip H. Powers, a cavalryman in the Army of Northern Virginia, wrote his wife,

"As Christmas will be pretty well over before you receive this, I need hardly wish you a Merry holiday. There is no holiday you will say for a poor woman with four children, a body full of ailments and pain and a husband in the rebel army... my mind has been much with you I have indeed wished and prayed that you might be comfortable and happy with our Richmond friends during the season, and have longed incessantly to be with you...I do not care to celebrate Christmas until I can do so with my children—and my wife—when will that holiday come?...I hope the children enjoyed themselves yesterday—I thought of them when I first awaked, and of their stockings—Fortunate for them they were in Richmond where something could be had from Santa Claus." [60]

Everyone struggled to provide some sort of Christmas for the children. Virginia mothers substituted sorghum or molasses for the sugar and spices they could no longer buy and made an ersatz gingerbread. John B. Jones, an antebellum author who worked as clerk to five Confederate war secretaries, was hardly the only Southern parent to discover that imagination went a long way toward merriment. He dragged out an old black chest that had not been opened in four years because they had lost the key. After trying twenty-five keys and a piece of wire, Jones forced the lock but did not lift the lid. On Christmas Day, he spun a fanciful tale for the children about a mysterious Old Black Chest.

> *"Immediately after its conclusion, the old chest was surrounded and opened, and among an infinite variety of rubbish were some articles of value, viz., of chemises (greatly needed), several pairs of stockings, 1 Marseilles petticoat, lace collars, several pretty baskets, 4 pair ladies' slippers (nearly new), and several books—one from my library, an octavo volume on Midwifery, 500 pages, placed there to prevent the children from seeing the illustrations, given me . . . more than twenty years ago. There were also many toys and keepsakes presented Mrs. J. when she was an infant, forty years ago, and many given our children when they were infants, besides various articles of infants' clothing, etc. etc., both of intrinsic value, and prized as reminiscences. The available articles, though once considered rubbish, would sell, and could not be bought here for less than $500. This examination occupied the family the remainder of the day and night— all content with this Christmas diversion—and oblivious of the calamities which have befallen the country. It was a providential distraction."* [61]

The Virginia open house tradition had, by this time, spread throughout the South. On at least two occasions, President and Mrs. Jefferson Davis held New Year's Day "levees" at the White House in Richmond. These were formal public receptions where the couple graciously received anyone who cared to come. "The President holds his first general levee on the first of January to which I hear everybody and his wife are going, there being a great many persons of high social position who have never seen him." [62] As the Armory Band played, presidential aides "with swords and sashes" announced each guest, who proceeded into the center parlor to be greeted by the President and his wife Varina. Afer being "received," visitors flowed slowly through the side drawing room and back outside through the front door. These New Year's Day levees lasted from three to four hours.[63]

By the middle of the nineteenth century, the transformation of Christmas was complete. Americans had purged the holiday of its behavioral excesses and recast it in a more wholesome format emphasizing families and children. Reformed, respectable, domesticated, Christmas flooded the country, finally seeping into the homes of the holdouts in western Virginia and in Puritan New England. The only excesses that worried parents were the commercial ones, the glut of toys and candy that threatened to spoil the youngsters and ruin the Christmas spirit. When the twentieth century dawned, nearly every home in America celebrated Christmas in some manner.

A Winslow Homer etching that appeared in the Christmas Day issue of <u>Harper's Weekly</u> in 1858 depicts the gathering of greens in the forest. Such scenes were common until the middle of the twentieth century.

CHRISTMAS FIRSTS

First known Christmas tree in Europe, Germany, 1605

First mention of wreaths in windows, Georgia, Moravian home, 1805

First poinsettia in the United States, 1828

First Christmas tree in Williamsburg, possibly in Virginia, 1842

First Christmas card, England, 1843

First department store Santa, Philadelphia, 1849

First president to have Christmas tree in White House, Franklin Pierce, 1856

First states to legalize Christmas as a holiday, Louisiana and Arkansas, 1831

First known Christmas tree dealer, New York, 1851

First American-made glass ornaments (glass balls and bead chains) by William DeMuth of New York, 1871

First patent for tree stand (three-legged iron holder), Hermann Albrecht and Abram C. Mott, 1876

First appearance of icicles made in Nuremberg of silver foil, 1878

First electric tree lights, developed in New York by Edward Johnson, 1882

First to import German tree ornaments, F. W. Woolworth in the 1880s

First ornament hooks developed, replaces tying onto tree, 1892

First commercial electric lights offered by General Electric, 1901

First Christmas tree farm, McGalliard, in New Jersey, 1901

First community Christmas tree, New York City 1912

First lighting of national Christmas tree on White House grounds, Calvin Coolidge, 1923

End Notes

1. Snyder, Philip, December 25<u>th</u>, p. xviii.

2. Lancaster <u>Intelligencer</u>, December 12, 1866, in Alfred L. Shoemaker, <u>Christmas in Pennsylvania</u>, p. 11.

3. The quotation and much of the information in this paragraph comes from volume I of <u>Cassell's Household Guide: A Complete Encyclopedia of Domestic and Social Economy</u>, p. 97-98.

4. Recollections of Julia Calvert Bolling Cabell, age 87, of Christmas, 1860, at Bolling Hall, Virginia.

5. Rawlings, Kevin, <u>We Were Marching on Christmas Day</u>, pp. 141-142. Rawlings' book is filled with first person accounts of Christmas during the Civil War, written by soldiers and civilians from both sides.

6. Restad, Penne, <u>Christmas in America</u>, p. 120.

7. Page, Thomas Nelson, <u>Social Life in Old Virginia Before the War</u>, p. 52.

8. Unpublished memoirs of Elizabeth Frances Gray, and <u>Cassell's Household Guide</u>, p. 98.

9. <u>Cassell's Household Guide</u>, p. 98.

10. Letter from Adam Foster to his daughter Cynthia, January 12, 1847.

11. Harriet Martineau describing a German Christmas tree in Boston in 1832, in Philip Snyder, "The Lighted Christmas Tree," <u>Antiques</u>, December 1975, p. 1142.

12. Hatch, Jane, <u>The American Book of Days</u>, p. 1145.

13. Miles, Clement, <u>Christmas in Ritual and Tradition</u>, p. 265.

14. Coffin, Tristam Potter, <u>The Illustrated Book of Christmas Folklore</u>, p. 75.

15. Dickens, Charles, "The Christmas Tree," <u>Christmas Books, Tales, and Sketches</u>, p. 359.

16. Both quotations found in George Johnson, <u>Christmas Ornaments, Lights, and Decorations</u>, p. 10.

17. <u>The Saturday Evening Post</u>, December 10, 1825, and Phillip V. Snyder, "The Lighted Christmas Tree," <u>Antiques</u>, December, 1975, p. 1143.

18. Interview in <u>Richmond News Leader</u>, December 25, 1928 by Martha Page Vandegrift, then 95, recalling her visit to the Tuckers for Christmas 1842; also Robert Scribner, "Virginia's 'German' Tree," <u>Virginia Cavalcade</u>, Winter 1956, pp. 4-7.

19. Stern, Philip VanDoren, <u>The Civil War Christmas Album</u>, p. 88.

20. Jones, John B. <u>A Rebel War Clerk's Diary</u>, p. 320.

21. Rulon, Philip R., <u>Keeping Christmas</u>, p. 94.

22. Stern, Philip VanDoren, ed., <u>The Civil War Christmas Album</u>, p. 61.

23. Ellen Mordecai recollects her childhood in Raleigh and Richmond in the 1830s in <u>Gleanings from Long Ago</u>, p. 17.

24. Tusser, Thomas, <u>Five Hundred Pointes of Good Husbandrie</u>, p. 68.

25. Coves, Elliott, ed., <u>The History of the Lewis and Clark Expedition</u>, p. 738.

26. Davis, Mrs. Jefferson, "Christmas in the White House," <u>Sunday World Magazine</u>, December 13, 1896.

27. December 26, 1864 diary entry of Judith Brockenbrough McGuire in <u>Diary of a Southern Refugee During the War</u>, p. 324.

28. <u>Calendar of Virginia State Papers</u>, Vol. IX, p. 430.

29. Coves, Elliott, ed., <u>The History of the Lewis and Clark Expedition</u>, p. 738 and 742.

30. Mordecai, Ellen, <u>Gleanings from Long Ago</u>, p. 17.

31. December 25, 1864 diary entry of John B. Jones in <u>A Rebel War Clerk's Diary</u>, pp. 466-67.

32. Snyder, Phillip, <u>December 25th</u>, p. 46.

33. December 25, 1862 diary entry of John B. Jones in <u>A Rebel War Clerk's Diary</u>, p. 141.

34. Poem written just after the Civil War by Morton Bryan Wharton, in collection of the United Daughters of the Confederacy, Richmond, VA.

35. Rawlings, Kevin, <u>We Were Marching on Christmas Day</u>, pp. 141-42.

36. Information on belsnickeling and shanghai-ing come from John L. Heatwole, <u>Holidays and Pastimes</u>, p. 52 and Katharine L. Brown, <u>Traditional Christmas Customs</u>, pp. 25-32.

37. Yetman, Norman R., <u>Life Under the "Peculiar Institution,"</u> p. 176.

38. Yetman, Norman R., <u>Life Under the "Peculiar Institution,"</u> p. 60; Roscoe E. Lewis, <u>The Negro in Virginia</u>, p. 87; and Charles L. Purdue, ed., <u>Weevils in the Wheat</u>, p. 229.

39. Farish, ed., <u>The Journal of Philip Vickers Fithian</u>, p.39.

40. Washington, Booker T., <u>Up From Slavery: An Autobiography</u>, p. 96.

41. Baird, Nancy Chappelear, ed., <u>Journals of Amanda Virginia Edmonds</u>, p. 9.

42. Lewis, Roscoe E., <u>The Negro in Virginia</u>, p. 87.

43. <u>Ibid.</u>, p. 87.

44. <u>Ibid.</u>, p. 78.

45. Rawlings, Kevin, <u>We Were Marching On Christmas Day</u>, pp. 79-80.

46. <u>Ibid</u>., p. 131.

47. Page, Thomas Nelson, <u>Social Life in Old Virginia Before the War</u>, p. 62.

48. Washington, Booker T., <u>Up From Slavery: An Autobiography</u>, p. 96.

49. <u>Ibid</u>., pp. 96-98.

50. Snyder, <u>December 25th</u>, p. 46.

51. <u>Cassell's Household Guide</u>, p. 371.

52. Harrison, Constance Cary, <u>Recollections Grave and Gay</u>, p. 170.

53. Letter of Mrs. Philip B. Cabell, age 87, recollecting Christmas 1860.

54. Baird, Nancy Chappelear, ed., <u>Journals of Amanda Virginia Edwards</u>, p. 64.

55. Rawlings, Kevin, <u>We Were Marching on Christmas Day</u>, p. 71.

56. Diary entry of December 25, 1861, <u>Mary Chesnut's Civil War</u>, p. 269.

57. The authors thank Kevin Rawlings, author of <u>We Were Marching on Christmas Day</u>, and Jim Blankenship, historian at the City Point Unit of the Petersburg National Battlefield, for their help with help with this photo and its possible identification. Quotation from Rawlings, pp. 133-34.

58. Stern, Philip VanDoren, <u>The Civil War Christmas Album</u>, p. 23.

59. Letter of December 30, 1863, from Phebe Yates Pember in <u>A Southern Woman's Story</u>, p. 131.

60. Rawlings, Kevin, <u>We Were Marching on Christmas Day</u>, p. 111.

61. Jones, John B., <u>A Rebel War Clerk's Diary</u>, pp. 466-67.

62. Pember, Phebe Yates, <u>A Southern Woman's Story</u>, p. 132.

63. The authors thank John and Ruth Ann Coski at the Museum of the Confederacy in Richmond for their help, which included the unpublished research report, "Social Life of the Confederate White House."

Photos courtesy of Colonial Williamsburg Foundation

Chapter Four

"Old England at its best"
A Twentieth-Century Virginia
Christmas

Christmas in the Old Dominion has long been painted with sentimental colors. Visitors from Europe found the celebrations enchanting. Americans in other states copied Virginia ways. Magazines and books about the holidays nearly always sketched an Old Virginia Christmas, a nostalgic look back at times and traditions that grew increasingly romantic as the years passed.

When the Bishop of Aberdeen returned home to Scotland in 1927, he gave a rhapsodic account of Christmas in Virginia.

> *"These dear Virginians! They are not Americans at all. They are just old fashioned English folk. One keeps wondering what on earth they are doing here. This is old England, old England at its best and kindliest. . . how delighted Charles Dickens would be with these Virginians. . . Every house is an open house. Everywhere flow the wassail bowls of that seductive Christmas beverage, `egg nog' which, in spite of the Volstead Act [Prohibition], surely contains more potent ingredients than whipped eggs and cream. How good it is to see the young folks dance, as handsome lads and as pretty girls as one could find in all the world. And to one's great surprise one finds great merriment in these early Victorian mid-day dinners, with Christmas presents on every plate and everyone down to the smallest schoolboy making a speech, and the grave leaders of the state compelled to wear a silly paper cap and play the*

fool. . . In front of the Capitol [Building in Richmond] stands a vast communal Christmas tree, rising 40 feet in height, blazing with colored lights and surrounded by shining star of Bethlehem. And almost every householder seems to have planted in his front garden his own Christmas tree, loaded with

Photo courtesy of Colonial Williamsburg Foundation

brilliant ornaments, while in every window hangs a holly wreath and a holly wreath on every door. . . I have never had such a jolly Christmas since the time when I was a boy. And the Virginia Christmas is not Christmas without Christ. Religion not only has a place but it has first place. Everywhere there are midnight eucharists and everywhere the churches are crowded on the morning of Christmas Day." [1]

The Virginia Christmas had not changed much in two hundred years. The open house of colonial days was still in vogue, as was the emphasis on parties, dancing, feasting, drinking, holly decoration and Christmas Day church services. The traditional Christmas box or tip to underlings had been transformed into wrapped gifts that passed from friend to friend and between family members. Firecrackers replaced the shooting of Christmas guns—at least in the cities. Decorated trees, indoors and on the lawn, now played a prominent role in the home and community. Commercially made tree ornaments had come on the market in the decades after the Civil War; still, many clung to the family tradition of making their own. There was no shortage of books to tell them how!

Christmas preparations—cooking, decorating, gift-giving, entertaining—fell largely within the woman's sphere. Indeed, references linking women to Christmas decorations go back at least as far as the 1500s when, in one English poem, women were urged to deck, or decorate, their houses for the holiday. "Get Iuye [ivy] and hull [holly], woman deck vp thyne house. . ." [2] Many

Photo courtesy of Colonial Williamsburg Foundation

A Christmas open house in 1946.

prints from the nineteenth century depict women buying holly boughs at the market and hanging garlands in the parlors. Those who wrote diaries or memoirs seldom fail to record their efforts during the holiday season.

Christmas was, of course, more virtuous if the decorations were hand-made. The polite fiction that all nicely brought up young ladies were artistic and clever with handicrafts drove this illusion.

> *"The days before Christmas were spent in cutting cedar pine boughs and holly for decoration. . . tie[ing] long lengths of string to make garlands," recalled one Richmond woman. "All windows had holly wreaths, and the pictures had sprigs of holly. . . The tying up of parcels with holly patterned papers tied with red ribbons and labelled was all important. . . Nearly everyone kept open house on Christmas which meant huge bowls of egg nog and fruit cake."* [3]

To make garlands, pieces of evergreen were tied one by one onto a length of heavy cord that was draped in festoons over the mantel. For an "over-door decoration," one book recommended that nails be driven through a wooden board to hold various fruits or gourds in position. Nuts and pine needles could be glued on next and the whole creation mounted over the door, usually on the inside. [4]

By the start of World War I, most American homes had a Christmas tree in the parlor. Its use, however, had changed. Once the tree had been the climax of the party, the moment when children gathered to admire its lighted branches and adults distributed the gifts, sweets, toys, and written verses tied onto its boughs. Now, instead of unveiling one's Christmas tree to an admiring crowd, families set it up on Christmas Eve or Christmas Day and left it on display for a few days. (Although today's miniature toy ornaments recall the old practice of tying toys onto the tree's sturdier branches.) Tabletop trees were a thing of the past. Floor-to-ceiling sizes replaced them. Handmade decorations and flags hung alongside commercially-made blown glass balls, often imported from Germany. Fastening the ornaments onto the boughs with string or thread became a lot simpler after 1892 when tree hooks were invented. But the most significant change was the introduction of electric lights.

Governor Elbert Lee Trinkle and his children enjoy Christmas 1925 in the Governor's mansion in Richmond. A few days later, young Billy lit a sparkler and accidentally ignited the dry tree. Within minutes, explosive flames had gutted much of the 1906 addition to this 1813 building. Tragedy was averted when an older boy and his mother jumped safely from a third story window. Note the unusual vertical placement of the strands of beads and tinsel roping on the tree.

Tree Lights

Tree lights were the one ornament that appeared on all Christmas trees. Most often, thin candles called tapers were wired to the tips of the branches, held upright—more or less—by a counterbalancing weight. Imaginative folks might make their own lights using walnut shells, egg shells, or pressed glass cups to hold a few drops of oil and a tiny wick. Those who could afford store-bought lighting might hang from the branches an assortment of tiny tin lanterns with candles inside or miniature oil lamps with little glass globes. One tree set up at a New York church in 1859 was lit by nearly two hundred gas jets!

The desire for safety fueled the search for less dangerous alternatives. The big break came with Edison's invention of the electric light bulb in 1879. Electricity came with its own risks—especially in the early years when it was a do-it-yourself effort—but it was far less dangerous than open flame. Within three years, the first electric tree lights appeared. Credit for the invention generally goes to Edward Johnson, an Edison colleague and vice-president of his electric company. At his house on New York's Fifth Avenue, Johnson rigged up an electrified, rotating Christmas tree that stunned visitors. (Notice that the colors first associated with tree lights were *not* red and green.)

Photo courtesy of The Library of Virginia

> *"It was brilliantly lighted with many colored globes about as large as an English walnut and was turning some six times a minute on a little pine box. There were 80 lights in all encased in these dainty glass eggs, and about equally divided between white, red, and blue. As the tree turned, the colors alternated, all the lamps going out and being relit at every revolution. The rest was a continuous twinkling of dancing colors, red, white, blue, white, red, blue—all evening."* [5]

By the 1890s, electric tree lights were all the rage among the well-to-do, who, after all, were the only people likely to have electrified homes and the money to spend on such innovation.

"No Danger! from the Lights on Christmas Trees when Edison Miniature Lamps are used" claims the advertisement in *Scientific American* magazine, above, at the turn of the century. The ads say that "Lamps can be either bought or rented at a low cost," but in truth, the lights were very expensive. So was the electricity needed to light them. A 1903 ad priced one string at $12, an average week's wages for a working man. The price soon fell—four years later Sears Roebuck offered them for $4.67—but lights were still beyond most American families. As for installation, "Any one can readily wire and put up the lamps if there is electric current in the house." [6]

Whatever the cost or degree of difficulty, Edison's Miniature Lamps enjoyed brisk sales from those who wanted to enjoy their tree without standing anxiously beside it with a bucket of water. By the 1920s, the increasing availability of electricity and its decreasing cost brought the price of electric tree lights within reach of the middle class.

The Community Christmas Tree

The invention of electric lights led, indirectly, to that singularly American Christmas custom known as the community Christmas tree. The very first was erected in 1912 in New York's Madison Square Garden. Crowds watched in wonder as men erected a 70-foot pine and then covered it with thousands of electric lights. Christmas carols in many different languages followed. Within a couple years, hundreds of cities across the country had followed the example, even in New England. No doubt our Puritan forefathers, who had once banned Christmas outright, groaned in their graves when that symbol of pagan ritual and frivolity went up on the Boston Common.

Williamsburg climbed on the community tree bandwagon in 1915. At the College end of the Duke of Gloucester Street, the town set up a large cedar tree. Church bells peeled, choirs sang, a prayer was offered, and the mayor switched on the lights to a chorus of happy exclamation. Over the next few years, the tree moved about town, from Palace Green (still called that even though the original Governor's Palace had burned in 1781 and been replaced by a school) to

Photo courtesy of Colonial Williamsburg Foundation

Williamsburg's Community Christmas tree as it appeared in 1946. Blackouts meant the lights could not be lit during the Second World War years.

Market Square Green near the Powder Magazine, then back to Palace Green. Finally it settled on a spot on Market Square where a large spruce grows in view of the site of Williamsburg's very first indoor Christmas tree in 1842. This living tree is still lit during a popular ceremony every year on Christmas Eve. But elsewhere, the custom fell out of favor and Community Christmas trees are seldom seen today.

A Williamsburg Christmas

At the dawn of the twentieth century, the overwhelming majority of Virginians still lived on the land. The War Between the States was recent history, kept alive by the ranks of aging veterans who could spin endless tales of Confederate heroism and the legions of maiden aunts who could talk "the good old days" until young eyes glazed over. Most Virginians held tight to their traditions, especially when it came to Christmas.

Christmas with the family was the tradition that mattered most. City dwellers who had country kinfolk rode wagons or trains "back home" for the holidays. Youngsters skated on icy ponds, hunted the woods for mistletoe and a suitable Christmas tree, shot off guns on Christmas and New Year's, and hung up the largest stockings they could find on Christmas Eve. Families gathered around the hearth to sing, laugh, tell stories, and share the joy of the season.

The Roaring Twenties mattered little to the Old Dominion but another sort of frenzy caught on during those years. History for sale, some called it, as wealthy northerners bought up dilapidated plantation homes and restored them to their former splendor. One New Yorker, John D. Rockefeller, Jr., bought up an entire town. It was the height of the Colonial Revival, a time when Americans looked to their country's formative years for inspiration, when styles of everything from furniture to architecture borrowed from the colonial, when genealogy flourished and monuments to the founding fathers were erected by the score. At the heart of this national movement was Virginia, "the birthplace of the nation," "the mother of presidents," and the home of most of the country's early leaders.

Virginia had already bequeathed the nation its old English Christmas traditions. Now, as the years of the twentieth century passed by, the Common-

wealth had another
Christmas gift for the
country, this one pack-
aged in historic
Williamsburg, wrapped
in candlelight and tied
with a sprig of holly. It
captured the longing for
a simpler time and re-
kindled the virtues of
family, self-reliance, and
hospitality that many
feared were dying out. It

John D. Rockefeller, Jr., left, leaving Bassett Hall, his Williamsburg home. Right, the Reverend W. A. R. Goodwin, rector of Bruton Parish Church, who persuaded Rockefeller to support the restoration of the colonial capital.

rejected the plastic commercialism that was threatening to overwhelm the holiday. Most people called it the "Williamsburg Christmas."

When Rockefeller's ambitious restoration of Williamsburg opened to the public in 1934, the interest in things colonial had never been greater. Visitors came by the thousands. They returned home inspired, and eager to bring a little of old Williamsburg into their own lives.

To the surprise of everyone in Williamsburg, visitors continued to visit during the Christmas holidays. No one had planned any Christmas activities or decorations. No one anticipated any visitors. The modern decorations that guests saw clashed sharply with the town's colonial serenity: evergreen trees strung with colored electric lights dotted the main street and red lights winked in the windows at the College of William and Mary. Williamsburg's Christmas was ill-matched to its time.

Those interested in historical accuracy pointed out that no evidence for outdoor Christmas decorations in the eighteenth century had ever been found and, consequently, decorations of all sort should be forbidden. But the Rever-end W.A.R. Goodwin, rector of Bruton Parish Church and the father of the restoration, spoke for many when he pointed out that Williamsburg was a living town, not a museum. Its citizens, he said, could hardly be expected to forego their Christmas customs for the sake of historical authenticity. A com-promise was struck between the twentieth century and the eighteenth:

Williamsburg would celebrate an old-fashioned Christmas, not a true colonial Christmas.

But how? Clearly, the newly restored colonial capital needed some outdoor Christmas decorations that were more compatible with its eighteenth-century character. In place of colored lights, an "illumination" was suggested. White candlelight would flicker in the windows of Williamsburg's four exhibition buildings and their entrances would be decorated with natural evergreen roping and wreaths. The entire cost of the effort, including the four custodians who were hired to keep the candles from burning down the restored buildings, came to fifty dollars.

Illumination was historically correct, although the practice had not usually been associated with Christmas during colonial times. Typically a single candle was lit high in the cupolas of public buildings or in the windows of private homes to commemorate an important battle or to celebrate a royal birthday. In 1702, for example, the windows of the College of William and Mary "were set with a double row of candles" during a ceremony to honor Queen Anne's ascension to the throne.[7] In 1774, Williamsburg was illuminated in honor of the arrival of Lady Dunmore, the governor's wife, who joined her husband from England. Shortly before Christmas, the *Virginia Gazette* reported an illumination at the Capitol Building in Williamsburg.

> *"Last night there was a ball and elegant entertainment at the Capitol, given by the Gentlemen of the Hon. the House of Burgesses to his Excellency the Governour, his Majesty's Council, and the Gentlemen and Ladies of this city, who were chiefly dressed in Virginia cloth, and made a genteel appearance. The Capitol was illuminated upon this occasion."* [8]

It was hoped that Williamsburg's private citizens would set aside their modern colored lights and join the illumination, creating a stunning but subdued ambience throughout the town. Announcements appeared in the local newspaper encouraging participation in the "White Lighting," but few complied. Lighted candles posed a real danger and it was necessary to stay at home while they burned. Money was an issue too—the cost of a new candle for each window every day for the week between Christmas Eve and New Year's Day was not insignificant during the Great Depression. And of course there were some people, like the Reverend W. A. R. Goodwin and President

John Stewart Bryan of the College, who simply preferred the look of colored lights.

Each year President Bryan decorated the windows of William and Mary's Wren Building with bright red electric lights, oblivious to the barrage of gentle hints from Colonial Williamsburg urging him to join the white light team. It was not until 1940 that the college president grudgingly gave in, but not before getting in the last word on the matter of authenticity.

> *"The College of William and Mary will be happy to cooperate with you and the colored lights will be removed," he wrote in a memo. "However, I would like to call your attention to the fact that I think red electric lights look better than white ones. Also I do not think of Christmas illumination in Colonial times. . . It is very interesting to have things historically correct but if Williamsburg is to have a real Colonial Christmas we had better buy some Arrak Punch, cut out Church services, and go to it in a historical way."*[9]

Electrified candles ultimately provided the solution to the safety problem, although until the late forties, the bulbs were sadly uncandle-like in appearance. The use of electrified candles was interrupted by the outbreak of World War II. Mandatory blackouts and the shortage of consumer goods caused by the war effort delayed bulb improvement for five years, but from then on, "faux" candles became an increasingly realistic alternative to candlelight.

Rudolph did not join Santa's reindeer team until shortly after World War II when the hit song by Johnny Marks was sung by Gene Autry, Bing Crosby, and many others.

Williamsburg stores that stocked up on the unusual candles found their inventories quickly depleted, not by locals, but by tourists charmed with the idea. In December of 1941, Casey's and Rose's department stores ordered 600 electric candles for local residents. By Christmas Eve, none remained. Quite unexpectedly, the Colonial Revival tradition called "White Lighting" was spreading westward from Williamsburg's Historic Area to the rest of the country.

Publicity generated by countless magazine and newspaper articles brought widespread attention. Merchants everywhere responded to customer demand for this inexpensive, understated, elegant form of holiday lighting. In some parts of the country, the style has become so entrenched that home builders design new houses with an illumination feature that lets the family turn on all the candles in the windows with one flick of a switch. Today, Williamsburg candlelight shines from the windows of homes in every state of the Union.

Decorated Wreaths

The ancient Greeks wore circular garlands of flowers or greens as a mark of honor; for the Romans, wreaths symbolized victory. Early Americans thought of wreaths—if they thought of them at all—in the same way. Not until the nineteenth century did anyone associate wreaths with Christmas. Their first known use during the holiday season appears in a 1805 reference to wreaths hanging in the windows (not on the door) of a Moravian home. Later in the century when the excessive abundance of the Victorian style reigned supreme, women hung up wreaths and garlands galore. For the most part, these remained indoor holiday decorations. Not until the twentieth century did magazines and decorating guides begin to encourage beautifying the *outside* of the house as well as the inside with wreaths of fresh evergreen or holly and bright red bows on the front door.

Photo courtesy of Colonial Williamsburg Foundation

The Governor's Palace in 1949 shows a tradition of simple yet impressive garlands and wreaths.

> *"We outline our doorways with trailing vines, pile the mantels with holly branches, and hang mistletoe in dim spots best suited to its usage, while every front door bears a beribboned wreath. . . wreaths may be hung on balconies as well as on doors, while bands of laurel and princess pine may outline the trim of entrances and windows."* [10]

The plain evergreen wreaths that decked the doors of Williamsburg's exhibition buildings in 1935 were in no way unusual for that time. The unusual would come the next year when the Williamsburg door decorations first bore fruit.

Thanks to a fad for the Renaissance artwork of Luca della Robbia and a Virginia floral decorator in Williamsburg, Christmas wreaths became a focal point for home decoration. Della Robbia's enameled terra cottas, with their fruited garlands and swags, inspired Christmas decorators to add shellacked fruit and vegetables, gilded pine cones, dried flowers, gold tissue, and ribbons to their wreaths and decorations.

> *"Of late years," wrote a magazine editor in 1926, "besides the staple wreaths of plain greens to which we have long been accustomed, the holiday's emblems have blossomed forth,—or perhaps we should say fruited forth,—with richness of color produced by the use of either natural or artificial fruit as embellishment."* [11]

Mrs. Louise Fisher, Williamsburg's "flower lady" who in 1936 had been placed in charge of Christmas decorating, admired the naturalism of the della Robbia style and thought it would fit well within the Williamsburg paradigm. She rejected anything plastic or shellacked in favor of the fruits and plants that had been available to colonial Virginians. Only natural materials would do. She began to look at English decorative examples, such as the carvings of Grinling Gibbons, for inspiration. And she hung her fruited wreaths *outside* on the front doors of the exhibition buildings.

Louise Fisher, who began at Colonial Williamsburg in 1936 as a hostess, pioneered the naturalistic "Williamsburg style" of Christmas decoration with her use of fresh fruits and historical plant material. She was influenced by the baroque wood carvings of English sculptor Grinling Gibbons and the terra cottas of the Renaissance Italian artist Luca della Robbia.

Never mind that no one in the eighteenth century would have been caught dead with real fruit tacked to his front door. Almost overnight, Mrs. Fisher's "della Robbia wreaths" became a sensation. In no time, everyone wanted a Williamsburg wreath on their door and a Williamsburg Christmas in their home. Professional florists fed the do-it-yourself market as early as the 1930s by supplying strong wire wreath frames wrapped with heavy green paper and stuffed with wet sphagnum moss. Magazines featured articles with instructions on making the fashionable Williamsburg door decorations. Mrs. Fisher and her growing staff gave demonstrations and provided directions through the mail. Colonial Williamsburg responded to public demand by selling nail-studded forms for making the more popular door decorations, especially the apple fan, right, that had been introduced in the 1970s, plus idea books, how-to books, and videos. Overnight, a cottage industry sprung up to instruct and supply homeowners with the necessary components for "Williamsburg" decorations.

Though it appears in at least one Christmas decorating manual from the 1930s, the apple fan mounted above the door was not introduced into Williamsburg until the 1970s. The interpretation of the apple fan created a minor sensation and flooded Colonial Williamsburg with requests for instructions.

But Mrs. Fisher and her staff only decorated Williamsburg's exhibition buildings. To encourage residents living inside the restored area to participate, a contest was held in 1937 and every year afterwards. Colonial Williamsburg provided basic materials, Mrs. Fisher offered instruction, and prizes went to the best decorated doors in town. The contest caught on at once. By 1940, it had expanded to four awards: Best Day

Ever since the first contest took place in 1937, visitors have poured into Williamsburg to admire the unique door decorations. In 1969, by popular demand, a Christmas decorations tour was started to answer visitors' questions about plant materials and share with them some of the construction techniques used to create these holiday arrangements. Many visitors are not aware that, while the professional landscaping staff decorates the exhibition buildings, taverns, and guesthouses, it is the individual residents who decorate their own homes each year and who vie for the blue ribbons awarded by the judges.

Decoration, Best Night, Best Outdoor Scene, and Best Illuminated. Rules were promulgated by the Williamsburg Garden Club and the awards presented at the Bonfire on Market Square. Many residents took it very seriously, and the blue ribbons affixed to the winning houses became a status symbol valued far more than any prize. Indeed, in 1940, a woman who won second place thanked the judges and promised to do better the next year! So many visitors poured into Williamsburg during the Christmas season to admire and photograph the door decorations that a "Garlands and Greens" tour was inaugurated in 1969.

The nature of Williamsburg's door decorations has changed a good deal over the decades. The gradual expansion of the holiday season from one week to six meant more use of longer-lasting dried plant materials, like cotton bolls, nuts, and pods, and fewer of the perishable fruits like pears that have to

Photos courtesy of Colonial Williamsburg Foundation

be replaced every few days. Conservation concerns led to the banning of running cedar and mountain laurel, which were facing wholesale destruction in the wild. Tastes changed, too. The pictorial scenes, above were popular in the early 1970's.

In the mid-1970's, authenticity requirements tightened. Instead of following the Italian della Robbia style (which had no real connection with colonial America), Colonial Williamsburg decorators looked also to English precedent in the works of Grinling Gibbons, a sculptor whose woodcarvings influenced colonial design. Certain plant materials, such as poinsettias, nandina, and pyracantha, were disqualified as too late for the colonial period because they had been introduced into Virginia after the eighteenth century. Bows and ribbons were forbidden as too Victorian.

More recently, symbols of the Historic Area trades have been incorporated into imaginative decorations. The shoemaker's shop uses strips of leather in the plaque next to his shop door, taverns tuck discarded oyster shells into their wreaths, and the cabinetmaker planes extra wood shavings to make decorative curls.

Some residents incorporate into their decorative scheme objects that give clues to the former use of their building. On the door of what once served as a laundry is a wreath of soap balls. The entrance to an eighteenth-century kitchen is decorated with a straw wreath and neatly-blown egg shells. At the Bluebell Tavern, playing cards and crossed clay pipes mark the front door. A nearby ordinary mixes tin mugs and citrus fruits to suggest holiday punch. John Greenhow's general store fastens tobacco twists onto twin wreaths. Six miles away on the James River at Carter's Grove Plantation, decorators use scallop shells collected along the riverbank to allude to this favorite holiday food.

Other related objects such as pheasant feathers, gingerbread boys, wooden spoons, red-checked napkins, marbleized paper, white porcelain wig curlers, straw toys, oyster shells, ribbon cockades, even clay bird bottles have come to play important roles in the story of Williamsburg decorations.

Today, from Maine to Miami, New York to New Mexico, Williamsburg's Colonial Revival decorations have become the country's most popular holiday decorating style. Homes in urban neighborhoods and retirement communities, suburbs and highrise apartment complexes, share the pleasures of this twentieth-century Virginia Christmas tradition.

Soon the Christmas season will be on us once again and Americans will celebrate the holidays in the American way: a little, a lot, or hardly at all, with whichever regional, religious, and ethnic traditions they chose. But those who welcome family and friends into their homes for a special holiday meal, who look forward to a day or a week off from work or school, who sing Christmas carols indoors and out and hang fresh greens in their homes and decorate "Williamsburg" doors, who take pleasure in serving that special punch or egg nog that grandmother used to make, who give gifts to children and tips to the people who provide them with services all year long, who hang mistletoe in the front hall and shoot off guns or firecrackers, who plan a wedding during the holiday season, who set electric candles in their windows, and who attend a church service and help decorate the sanctuary—all those Americans are celebrating a Virginia Christmas. And they are celebrating in much the same way as people have been celebrating for the past four centuries.

"When Christmas is done, kepe not Christmas time still."
—Thomas Tusser, 1557

End Notes

1. Newspaper clipping, 1927, in "Social Life and Customs: Virginia Christmas" folder at Valentine Museum in Richmond.
2. Tusser, Thomas, <u>Five Hundred Pointes of Good Husbandrie</u>, p. 225; and the <u>Oxford English Dictionary</u>.
3. Unpublished memoirs of Nancy Keene Perkins Lancaster.
4. Hottes, Alfred C., <u>1001 Christmas Facts and Fancies</u>, p. 86, 96-99.
5. Johnson, George, <u>Christmas Ornaments, Lights, and Decorations</u>, p. 17.
6. Ads from <u>Scientific American</u>, November 23, 1901, p. 338; November 30, 1901, p. 356; December 7, 1901, p. 372; December 14, 1901, p. 404. Other ads cited in Philip Snyder, "The Lighted Christmas Tree," <u>Antiques</u>, December 1975, p. 1145; and George Johnson, <u>Christmas Ornaments, Lights, and Decorations</u>, p. 145.
7. "The Journal of Francis Louis Michel," <u>Virginia Magazine of History and Biography</u>, April 1916, p. 128.
8. <u>Virginia Gazette</u>, December 14, 1769.
9. Letter from William and Mary President Bryan, dated December 10, 1940.
10. Russell, Elizabeth, "Wreaths and Swags," <u>House Beautiful</u>, p. 695.
11. <u>Ibid</u>., p. 695.

Photo courtesy of Colonial Williamsburg Foundation

Acknowledgments

The authors would like to thank everyone who helped with the research, photography, and design of this book, particularly Cathy Grosfils, Dave Doody, Kathryn Arnold, and Tom Greene at Colonial Williamsburg, Teresa Roane at The Valentine Museum of the Life and History of Richmond, Dale Wheary at Maymont Foundation, Carolyn Parsons, Ruth Ann Coski, and John Coski at the Museum of the Confederacy, Audrey Johnson at the Library of Virginia, Rhonda Howdyshell and Alex Tillen at the Frontier Culture Museum, Randy Hackenburg at the U.S. Army Military History Institute, Sylvia Evans at the Wilton House Museum, Jim Blankenship at the Petersburg National Battlefield, City Point Unit, and also Kevin Rawlings, Bill Apperson and Mrs. Robert S. Barlow; also the indefatigable reference librarians at the Virginia Historical Society, the Library of Virginia, the Tuckahoe Public Library, and the Colonial Williamsburg Library. Special thanks go to the people who helped turn the manuscript into a book: Wert Smith, Robert Dietz, and Katrina Jordan of The Dietz Press.

Bibliography

Four Centuries
of Virginia Christmas

Alberts, Robert C. *The Golden Voyage.* Boston: Houghton Mifflin Co., 1969.

Arber, Edward and A. G. Bradley, editors. *Travels and Works of Captain John Smith.* Edinburg: John Orant, 1910.

Baird, Nancy Chappelear. *Journals of Amanda Virginia Edmonds: 1859-1867.* Stephens City, VA: Commercial Press, 1984.

Barbour, Philip L. ed. *The Complete Works of Captain John Smith,* Volume II. Chapel Hill, NC: University of North Carolina Press, 1986.

Belden, Louise C. *The Festive Tradition: Table Decoration and Desserts in America, 1650-1900.* New York: W. W. Norton & Co., 1983.

Beverley, Robert. *History and Present State of Virginia.* Louis B. Wright, ed. Chapel Hill, NC: University of North Carolina Press, 1947.

Bond, Donald F., ed. *The Spectator.* Oxford: 1965.

Brown, Katharine L. *Traditional Christmas Customs.* Staunton, VA: American Frontier Culture Foundation, 1997.

Cabell, Mrs. Philip B. (Julia Calvert Bolling). Unpublished recollections of Christmas 1860, at the Virginia Historical Society, Richmond, VA.

Calendar of Virginia State Papers, Volume IX. Richmond: 1890.

Carson, Jane. *Colonial Virginians at Play.* Williamsburg, VA: Colonial Williamsburg Foundation, 1989.

Cassell's Household Guide: A Complete Encyclopedia of Domestic and Social Economy. London: Cassell, Petter, and Galpin, ca. 1875.

Chinard, Gilbert, ed. *A Huguenot Exile in Virginia: The Journal of Durand of Dauphine, 1687.* New York: Press of the Pioneers, 1934.

The Christmas Book: Christmas in the Olden Time: its Customs and their Origin. London, 1859.

Coffin, Tristam Potter. *The Illustrated Book of Christmas Folklore.* New York: Seabury Press, 1973.

Coves, Elliott, ed. *The History of the Lewis and Clark Expedition*. New York: Dover, n.d.

Cox, James A. "Saving Christmas in the Colonies," *Colonial Williamsburg Journal*, Winter 1990-1991.

Cresswell, Nicholas. *Journal of Nicholas Cresswell*. New York: Dial Press, 1928.

Davis, Mrs. Jefferson. "Christmas in the White House," *Sunday World Magazine*, December 13, 1896.

DelRe, Gerard and Patricia. *Christmas Almanack*. New York: Doubleday, 1979.

Dennison's Christmas Book: Decorations and Novelties for Use in Homes, Halls, Clubs, School-rooms and Churches. Boston: Dennison Manufacturing Co., 1921.

DeSimone, David. "Another Look at Christmas in the Eighteenth Century," *Colonial Williamsburg Interpreter*, Winter 1995-1996.

DeSimone, David. "The Christmas Box Tradition," *Colonial Williamsburg Interpreter*, Winter 1997.

DeSimone, David. "Christmas in Revolutionary Times," *Colonial Williamsburg Interpreter*, Winter 1996-1997.

Dickens, Charles. "The Christmas Tree" (1850), *Christmas Books, Tales and Sketches*. Garden City, New York: Nelson Doubleday, n.d.

Farish, Hunter Dickinson, ed. *The Journal of Philip Vickers Fithian*. Williamsburg, VA: Colonial Williamsburg Foundation, 1957.

Foley, Daniel J. *Christmas in the Good Old Days*. Philadelphia: Chilton Co., 1961.

Ford, Paul Leicester, ed. *The Writings of Thomas Jefferson*. New York: G. P. Putnam's Sons, 1894.

Foster, Adam. Unpublished letter to daughter, Jan. 12, 1847, at the Virginia Historical Society, Richmond, VA.

Gelman, Barbara, ed. *The Wood Engravings of Winslow Homer*. New York: Bounty Books, 1969.

Gill, Harold. "Christmas in Colonial Virginia," *Colonial Williamsburg Journal*, October/November, 1999.

Glasse, Hannah. *The Complete Confectioner*. London: 1770.

Godey's Lady's Book. December, 1850, December, 1860, December 1862.

Goodwin, Mary R. M. "Christmas in Colonial Virginia." Williamsburg, VA: unpublished Colonial Williamsburg Foundation Research Report, 1955.

Goodwin, Mary R. M. "Historical Notes: The College of William and Mary," unpublished Colonial Williamsburg Research Report, 1954.

Gray, Elizabeth Frances. Unpublished memoirs at the United Daughters of the Confederacy, Richmond, VA.

Harris, Brayton. "Christmas," *Virginia*, Winter 1993.

Harrison, Constance Cary. *Recollections Grave and Gay*. New York: Charles Scribner's Sons, 1911.

Hatch, Jane M. *The American Book of Days*. New York: Wilson, 1978.

Heatwole, John L. *Holidays and Pastimes*. Berryville, Virginia: Rockbridge Publications, 1998.

Hottes, Alfred C. *1001 Christmas Facts and Fancies*, New York: Dodd, Mead & Co., 1937.

Howell, Wendy. "Setting a Fine Table: The Christmas Season," *Colonial Williamsburg Interpreter*, Winter 1996-1997.

Johnson, George. *Christmas Ornaments, Lights, and Decorations*. Paducah, KY: Collector Books, 1987.

Jones, Hugh. *The Present State of Virginia.* London: 1724.

Jones, John B., *A Rebel War Clerk's Diary.* Edited by Earl Schenck Miers. New York: A. S. Barnes & Co., Inc., 1961.

Kainen, Ruth Cole. *America's Christmas Heritage.* New York: Funk & Wagnalls, 1969.

Lancaster, Nancy Keene Perkins. "Christmas of Youth," unpublished memoir ca. 1905-1915 in Virginia Historical Society.

Lee, Harry. "Christmas?" *Country Life,* December 1919.

Lewis, Roscoe E. *The Negro in Virginia.* New York: Hastings House, 1940.

Lockridge, Kenneth A., ed. *The Diary and Life of William Byrd II of Virginia, 1674-1744.* Chapel Hill: University of North Carolina Press, 1987.

London Magazine, 1746.

McGuire, Judith Brockenbrough. *Diary of a Southern Refugee During the War.* New York: E. J. Hale & Son, 1867.

Michel, Francis Louis. "The Journal of Francis Louis Michel, 1702," edited by William J. Hinke. *Virginia Magazine of History and Biography,* April 1916.

Miles, Clement. *Christmas in Ritual and Tradition.* London: T. Fisher Unwin, 1912.

Mordecai, Ellen. *Gleanings from Long Ago.* Raleigh, NC: Mordecai Square Historical Society, Inc., 1974.

Mordecai, Samuel. *Richmond in By-Gone Days.* Richmond, VA: Dietz Press, 1946.

Morpurgo, J. E. *Their Majesties' Royall Colledge.* Washington, D.C.: Hennage Creative Printers, 1976.

Nissenbaum, Stephen. *The Battle for Christmas.* New York: Alfred A. Knopf, 1996.

Noel Hume, Ivor. "'Twas the Day After Christmas," *Colonial Williamsburg Journal,* Autumn 1997.

Olmert, Michael. "The Hospitable Pineapple," *Colonial Williamsburg Journal,* Winter 1997-98.

Oxford English Dictionary. Oxford: Clarendon Press, 1961.

Page, Thomas Nelson. *Social Life in Old Virginia Before the War.* Sandwich, MA: Chapman Billies Inc., 1994.

Pember, Phebe Yates. *A Southern Woman's Story: Life in Confederate Richmond.* Edited by Bell Irvin Wiley. Marietta, GA: Mockingbird Press, 1974.

Perdue, Charles L. Jr. et al., editors. *Weevils in the Wheat.* Charlottesville: University Press of Virginia, 1976.

Powers, Emma L. "'Tis the Season," *Colonial Williamsburg Interpreter,* Fall 1999.

Putnam, Sallie B. *Richmond During the War; Four Years of Personal Observation by a Richmond Lady.* New York: G. W. Carleton & Co., 1867; reprinted by Time-Life, 1983.

Raffald, Elizabeth. *The Experienced English Housekeeper.* London: 1775.

Rawlings, Kevin. *We Were Marching on Christmas Day: A History and Chronicle of Christmas During the Civil War.* Baltimore, MD: Toomey Press, 1995.

Restad, Penne L. *Christmas in America.* New York: Oxford University Press, 1995.

Roberts, F. *Round about our Coal-Fire.* London: F. Roberts, ca.1740.

Rulon, Philip R. *Keeping Christmas.* Hamden, CT: Archon Books, 1990.

Russell, Elizabeth. "Wreaths and Swags," *House Beautiful,* December 1926.

Scientific American Magazine. Advertisements in issues November 23, 1901, November 30, 1901, December 7, 1901, December 14, 1901.

Scribner, Robert L. "Virginia's 'German' Tree," *Virginia Cavalcade,* Winter 1956.

Shoemaker, Alfred L. *Christmas in Pennsylvania*. Kutztown, PA: Pennsylvania Folklife Society, 1959.

Smith, E. *The Compleat Housewife*. London: E. Smith, 1758.

Snyder, Philip V. "The Lighted Christmas Tree," *Antiques*, December 1975.

Snyder, Philip. *December 25th*. New York: Dodd, Mead & Co., 1985.

Snyder, Philip. *The Christmas Tree Book*. New York: Viking Press, 1976.

"Social Life and Customs: Virginia Christmas" folder at Valentine Museum, Richmond, VA.

Sterling, Mrs. B. B. Unpublished memoirs at the United Daughters of the Confederacy, Richmond, VA.

Stern, Philip VanDoren. *The Civil War Christmas Album*. New York: Hawthorn Books Inc., 1961.

Tille, Alexander. *Yule and Christmas, Their Place in the Germanic Year*. London: David Nutt, 1899.

Turner, John. "A Sedate, Rational, and Manly Pleasure," *Colonial Williamsburg Interpreter*, Winter 1998-1999.

Turner, John. "Freeing Religion Resource Book." Williamsburg, VA: unpublished Colonial Williamsburg Research Report, 1998.

Turner, John. "Hark! How All the Welkin Rings," *Colonial Williamsburg Interpreter*, Winter 1998-1999.

Tusser, Thomas. *Five Hundred Pointes of Good Husbandrie*. (1580 edition collated with those of 1573 and 1577). Edited by W. Payne and Sidney Herrtage. London: Trubner and Co., 1878. (Vaduz: Kraus Reprint, 1965).

Virginia Almanack, 1764, 1766, 1771, 1776.

Virginia Gazette. Purdie & Dixon, editors. December 14-21, 1739; February 25, 1768; December 14, 1769; December 28, 1769.

Warren, Nathan B. *The Christmas Book: Christmas in the Olden Time*. London: J. Pattie, 1859.

Washington, Booker T. *Up From Slavery: An Autobiography*. USA: Doubleday & Co., Inc., 1963.

Wharton, Morton Bryan. Unpublished poem in the United Daughters of the Confederacy, Richmond, VA.

Woodward, C. Vann, ed. *Mary Chesnut's Civil War*. New Haven: Yale University Press, 1981.

Wust, Klaus. *The Virginia Germans*. Charlottesville, VA: University Press of Virginia, 1969.

Yetman, Norman R. *Life Under the "Peculiar Institution": Selections from Slave Narrative Collection*. New York: Holt, Rinehart & Winston, Inc. 1970.

Index

Four Centuries
of Virginia Christmas